Alborough De Burgh

ELIZABETH

The Empress of Austria

MEISTERSPRUNG

ISBN-10: 153717780X / ISBN-13: 978-1537177809

NEW EDITION. ORIGINAL TEXT. 18 PHOTOGRAPHS
THE BOOK WAS FIRST PUBLISHED IN 1899. THE PUBLISHER DOES NOT
WARRANT THAT THE NEW EDITION IS COMPLETE AND CORRECT. IN NO
EVENT WILL THE PUBLISHER, ITS EMPLOYEES OR ITS PARTNERS BE
LIABLE FOR ANY DECISION MADE OR ACTION TAKEN IN RELIANCE ON
THE NEW EDITION OR FOR ANY CONSEQUENTIAL, SPECIAL OR SIMILAR
DAMAGE, EVEN IF ADVISED OF THE POSSIBILITY OF SUCH DAMAGE. THE
NEW EDITION SHALL NOT BE USED FOR ANY OFFICIAL OR SCHOLAR
PURPOSE.

PUBLISHED BY MEISTERSPRUNG LITERATUR 2016
MANUFACTURED AND DISTRIBUTED BY AMAZON.COM

BOOK COVER: EMPRESS ELIZABETH OF AUSTRIA

PREFACE.

When I undertook to write a memoir of the late Empress of Austria, I was fully aware of the great difficulties I should encounter, especially as the material I had collected from various quarters was enormous, and I felt it to be my duty to sift it thoroughly and to select only such parts as I could myself believe to be authentic. I have personally had the happiness of meeting the illustrious lady who is the subject of my sketch; I have seen her on many occasions and followed with interest the vicissitudes of her life for the last thirty years; I have often had occasion to write about her, and have also had the privilege of knowing some of those who were in her entourage and who, from time to time, have given me news, anecdotes, and reminiscences of the woman they loved with all their heart and soul.

EMPRESS ELIZABETH OF AUSTRIA.

In respect to Chapters XIII. and XIV., the various reports I have had from eye-witnesses coincide so fully with those published at the time in the daily press, that I have largely quoted from them, and have used principally the reports as they appeared in the Daily Telegraph.

CONTENTS.

INTRODUCTION.

When years hence the historian will chronicle the events of the nineteenth century, he will have to record many tragedies which have befallen personages who were prominently before the public - murders and suicides of reigning monarchs or heirs to crowns and of men chosen to preside over the destinies of nations, the sudden deaths of many born to the purple under the saddest circumstances, and the fall of mighty thrones; he will have to speak of revolutions and rebellions, of bloody deeds committed by members of secret societies, and of cruel wars, becoming more terrible every year as the inventive spirit of our time succeeds in the construction of machinery for the wholesale destruction of mankind.

And amongst the array of tragedies he will have to record the murder of a woman who, though occupying an exalted position, was essentially a friend of the people, and especially of the poor, the miserable, and the suffering, with whom she was ever in sympathy, and for whom she seemed to live.

The writing of the life-story of the late Empress Elizabeth of Austria, Queen of Hungary, is to me a labour of love: I have ever admired her as I saw her pass through the different stages of her career; I have had many times the privilege of seeing and observing her and her doings; I have felt for her the most sincere sympathy in the times of her suffering, she has had my heart-felt good wishes in the time of her joy; I have been fully aware of her unostentatious work of benevolence; I have closely followed her many deeds of generosity and unselfishness, and of many of them I have become personally cognisant; I have seen her making the woes of others her own, and doing all in her power to alleviate the grief and pain of her neighbours, were they her own people, or were they strangers - her kindness of heart knew no limits.

Is it not an appalling irony of life, that the beautiful and lonely Empress, who for so many years had wandered from place to place doing good - who, remote from all the distractions of politics and

5

Court life, herself scourged by so many unspeakable sorrows, only seeking for peace and rest for her troubled soul, appealing to the sympathy of mankind - should have been assassinated in cold blood by an obscure ruffian, who had no other grudge against her but that he hated all whose position was better than his own?

It is never an easy task to write a biography of any one who has just departed this life; and it becomes especially difficult when one feels that one cannot do full justice to the subject, that it is impossible to adequately describe a life so beautiful, so interesting, as that which I shall try to represent in this memoir.

It would be difficult to find any woman in this century who has been overwhelmed by such terrible events as those that mercilessly followed the late Empress; and to say this means much, for there are now living some women who have not only lost their beloved ones, but their thrones as well.

I have endeavoured in one of the chapters of this work to crowd into a limited space the misfortunes of the late Empress of Austria: naturally I can only speak of a few of the more important ones. As an affectionate wife she shared, as a matter of course, all the troubles and worries of her imperial spouse, and felt it ever her duty to stand by him with consolation and love, and so make less bitter the cup it was his fate to drink.

Nothing can be more characteristic and pathetic than her description of her condition of mind to one of her intimates some years ago. „When one has no wish to live longer," she said, „one is in reality not alive."

Then she added: „There is in life for every one a moment when he dies inwardly, and it is not necessary that this should happen only at the death of the body."

The love that she had for her son, and the hope that had centred in his career, were indescribable. What his terrible death meant to her is expressed in her own words just quoted; her heart was slain.

Undoubtedly the Empress had the strange temperament of the Wittelsbach family to which she belonged; by this the intense sympathy that existed between her and King Ludwig, her cousin, may be explained - it could only spring from a certain sense of kinship of spirit.

One of our great psychologists remarked, as the outcome of long observations, „The unhappy flee where no man pursueth." And so it was with poor Elizabeth; she appeared haunted and chased by sad memories, by the phantoms of past hopes and dead affections, and she became a wanderer, seeking in vain for rest.

Her sense of duty was strongly developed, and her liberal ideas have certainly done much to shed lustre upon the era of Francis Joseph. It is true she rarely took any part in politics; but she improved the social reputation of her Court, and in no small measure contributed to the extraordinary popularity of the Emperor, having greatly assisted him in winning the love and attachment of his heterogeneous subjects; and no one has acknowledged this more readily than Francis Joseph himself.

It was a fact especially observable in Elizabeth, that whenever called upon to become the consoler of her husband her strength never failed her; and however terrible the reaction may have been afterwards, she was always ready to stand by his side, when it became necessary either to impart to him grievous news or to encourage him in the bearing of them.

The Empress-Queen had been all her life a staunch adherer of the Roman Catholic Church; she hardly ever passed a day without hearing Mass, and she ever found great consolation in her religion; but by no means was she narrow-minded, and amongst her greatest friends she numbered Protestants, Jews, and even Mohammedans. As we are aware, she had just come from a visit to her friend the Baroness Rothschild, who has a most charming villa on the shore of Lake Leman, when she fell a victim to the murderer's steel. In her deeds of benevolence she knew no creed - all sufferers were alike to her; and perhaps in that very fact she showed that she was a true follower of the Great Teacher.

CHAPTER I.

THE PRINCESS ELIZABETH OF BAVARIA.

On the shores of the Lake of Starenberg, not far from the Bavarian capital, Munich, in the midst of a charming landscape of mountain and vale, surrounded by a park and beautiful gardens, bordering on picturesque forests of beech trees, there stands the Castle of Possenhofen, which nestles on the lake side among the roses and flowers which have made those regions renowned. This castle was once the home of the late Empress of Austria. Duke Maximilian of Bavaria and his wife lived here the life of a country squire and squiress, happy in the midst of a family of boys and girls, some of whom have been called to fill most exalted positions, and whose names have become well known for their intrepid deeds, their physical strength and endurance and philanthropy.

Today the visitor to the castle and park will be reminded of some of the romances which occurred among the shady avenues and beautiful rose gardens of this charming spot; he will see before his mind's eye the sprightly Princess Elizabeth, her more serious elder sister Helen, the younger happy children chasing each other through the avenues and rose walks of the gardens, and the boys playing the games of happy childhood.

It is reported that Elizabeth was the favourite child of her father, and his constant companion on his excursions in the mountainous districts. Duke Maximilian was a scientist and student; but he did not disdain recreations, and found happiness in moving amongst the peasants of his neighbourhood, to whom he often would play on his zither, frequently accompanied by his daughter Elizabeth. The girl grew up a lover of nature, a child of the woods, loving to wander about on the mountain sides or racing a pony along the shores of the lake. She had the happiest of childhoods, being allowed to run wild with her brothers amongst the Bavarian Alps, where she learned to ride and row and run as they did, and formed that taste for athletic exercises which distinguished her through life. She was troubled little with education, and in later years would laughingly declare that at that time she was the most ignorant princess in Europe, as she knew nothing save the rudiments of some half-dozen languages and what she had picked up at the knee of her father. I need not say that her modesty was somewhat exaggerated.

The Duchess Ludovica, Elizabeth's mother, and sister of the Archduchess Sophie, mother of Francis Joseph, was a proud, ambitious woman, and had centred all her hopes on her eldest daughter, whom she had resolved should be Empress of Austria; and when some duenna approached her with the information that the Duchess Elizabeth was masquerading with her brothers, and had played the zither on the hill side while the peasants danced to the strains of her instrument, or had been belated in the mountains and had spent the night in a deserted hut, Her Royal Highness would smile indifferently, and say she would take the child in hand later on, but for the present was too much occupied to attend to her.

How the young Princess loved to climb the rugged peaks of the Alps, and to gather the Edelweiss and other Alpine flowers, is still related amongst the peasantry of the district. She was not devoted to study, which seemed slow to her; she preferred the lessons she received from observation and contemplation of nature itself. As a matter of fact she was not brought up to fill the exalted position to which she was afterwards called; and but for her graceful beauty Elizabeth of Bavaria would certainly have escaped the notice of her cousin, the then young Emperor of Austria, whose troth was currently reported to be pledged to her elder sister, Helen. Elizabeth's marriage was a love match, at any rate on one side, and most likely on both; and that it proved a most beneficent one for the Emperor is well known, and has frequently been confirmed by himself in addresses to his subjects. However this may be, no young princess declines the hand of such an emperor as Francis Joseph. Never, even among the most romantic of the romantic middle classes - for it is a libel to say that middle-class young people are not romantic - was a young fellow so much in love with his fiancee as was Francis Joseph with his sixteen-year-old bride. The Emperor nourished the most passionate and chivalrous devotion for the beautiful Elizabeth, whom he had discovered for himself without the aid of ambassador or foreign minister, as he used laughingly to boast to members of his house, when there was a question of this alliance or that being arranged for him by the diplomatic statesmen. It needed all his love, however, to reconcile his highspirited youthful consort to her new position.

Duke Maximilian was in the habit of spending the winter at his beautiful palace in Munich, but Elizabeth was never happy there. Although the apartments were of large dimensions and beautifully adorned with frescoes by Kaulbach, the Princess always thought them narrow; she often said that she could not breathe in those small rooms, and used to enjoy principally to run about in the large riding school which was attached to the palace. Here she loved what she called „playing circus." She mounted and rode the most restive and unmanageable horses, and did not seem to know what fear was. Once she was thrown by one of the blood horses; a cry of terror sounded through the arena; but the little Duchess, not in the least frightened, jumped up from the ground where she had landed, and smilingly begged to be allowed to mount the horse again, which wish was not granted by her frightened governess.

The Duchess Ludovica was a sister of King Ludwig I. of Bavaria, and was for more than fifty years the popular and universally beloved mistress of Possenhofen. She was highly intellectual, well known for her wit and intelligence, and it was no doubt due to the fact that she personally undertook to superintend the education of her children that they all displayed a great love for science and art. Princess Elizabeth Amalie Eugenie, the late Empress, was the second daughter of Duke Maximilian and his wife Ludovica Maria, and was born on the 24th of December, 1837 - a date which is considered to be of ill omen in many parts of the world. As already mentioned, her father devoted his life to the study of natural history, national economy, and history. Both Princess „Lisel," as the late Empress was called, and her eldest brother, Ludwig, were quite different from the other members of the family; they were full of life and wit, but the others were serious and studious.

Princess Elizabeth was considered a dreamer, like her second brother, Charles Theodore. She was such a sensitive and affectionate child that both parents could not help spoiling her to a very great extent; but from her very first youth she showed a great predilection for the pleasures nature can offer and for country life. When but little over fifteen years of age, she undertook her first journey. With her mother and her sisters she went to Ischl to spend the summer, where the parents of Francis Joseph also had their summer residence. It was rumoured that the visit of the ducal family was not without purpose, and the Duchess was fondly hoping to see the crown of an empress placed upon the brow of her eldest daughter, Helen.

On the 16th of August, 1853, a most lovely summer day, the Emperor appeared quite unexpectedly at that popular summer resort. Although it was his habit to spend a month there every year with his parents, his unlooked-for arrival embarrassed the Bavarian ladies not a little, as they were apparently not prepared with the necessary wardrobe for the reception of so exalted a guest, and everything possible was done to furnish Princess Helen with such finery as would suit her high position and make her appear at her best.

Elizabeth had been out for a walk, and, returning, entered unannounced, as usual, the apartments of her aunt, the Archduchess Sophie, the mother of Francis Joseph, where she always found some dainties prepared for her special delectation. Her cheeks the colour of a sun-kissed peach, a large bouquet of wild flowers in her hand, she ran into the salon; without the slightest embarrassment she immediately recognised the Emperor from the portraits she had seen, and, running up to him, she exclaimed in a clear child's voice, „God greet thee, cousin!"

The Emperor was enchanted by the charming apparition; and when Princess Helen, decked out to perfection, entered the salon, she was too late - the Emperor of Austria had neither hand nor heart to bestow upon her.

On the same evening a carriage arrived at the villa to take a party out for a drive to a near-lying village. The Emperor placed a shawl upon his mother's shoulders, and at the same time slipped off from her arm a diamond bangle which she wore, whispering to her, „This we shall lay under Elizabeth's serviette at tea." The Archduchess Sophie at once understood the situation; she did not put a single question to her son; and when the next morning the Archduchess went to Mass with her Bavarian relatives, she stepped back at the door and allowed Princess Elizabeth to enter first. That was a public announcement of the great event more pronounced than if it had been given out in the Official Gazette.

But when the Mass was ended the youthful Emperor took the child-Princess Elizabeth by her hand and led her up to the altar, and meeting the officiating priest as he came down the steps, said to him, „Pastor, please bless us; this is my intended bride." On the 23rd of August the Vienna Gazette published the first official news of the betrothal.

The Duchess Helen of Bavaria married afterwards the Prince of Thurn and Taxis, and died eight years ago; her son, the present Prince Albert, is married to an Austrian archduchess, known in England as an authoress, having published in English a well-known work on the Austrian mountain districts, and who has one son, Prince Francis Joseph.

The betrothal of the sixteen-year-old Princess Elizabeth to the Emperor, who was twenty-three and a man of extreme good looks and figure, was very popular, both in Bavaria and Austria. It is generally accepted as a fact that the young bride was at that time the most beautiful princess in Christendom. It is told that, when Elizabeth was informed that she should be Empress, she exclaimed, „It cannot be possible; I am such an insignificant little thing"; but when her aunt assured her that Francis Joseph was absolutely in earnest, and would have no other wife but „Lisel," she joyfully accepted the Emperor-King's proposal, and three days afterwards the betrothal of the young couple was solemnly consecrated in the palace chapel of Ischl. Eight months later they were wedded at St. Augustine's by the Prince Archbishop of Vienna amidst public rejoicings, in which the whole population of Austria participated, the City Council giving general expression of its loyal gladness by liberally dowering forty penniless brides whose nuptial rites were celebrated on the day of the imperial wedding.

When the Emperor, shortly after his betrothal, met Count O'Donnell, who had saved his life at the time the insane Libenye had attempted to murder him, he addressed the young Austro-Irish officer thus: „In my happiness I today thank you again with all my heart that you have saved my life."

At the time the betrothal became known at Ischl, the people seemed almost unable to show sufficiently their joy and happiness over the event. On the young Emperor returning with his bride one night from an excursion from Hallstadt, the whole town was magnificently illuminated; the Austrian and Bavarian colours were gracefully intertwined, and thousands upon thousands of lamps were placed along the roads and streets and promenades; and from the heights and peaks of the surrounding mountains beacons threw their glare, and upon the highest peak of all a temple in beautiful classic style, surmounted by an imperial crown over the united initials of the royal bridegroom and bride, was traced out in many-coloured lamps, which showed their radiance for miles around.

The winter following his engagement the young sovereign frequently visited Munich, where his bride sojourned; and the populace of the Bavarian capital testified by their many ovations and demonstrations of joy how pleased they were that one of the daughters of their own country should be selected to be the first Catholic lady of Europe and consort of the proudest of its rulers. The Emperor's last visit to Munich was on the 9th of March, 1854. When he left the ducal palace eight days later in an open carriage drawn by six horses, to commence his journey back to Vienna, he stood up in his carriage, and looked back to the upper storey of the residence, where there stood at the window in all her radiant beauty and youth the woman who was in future to share joy and grief with him. Taking off his military cap and swinging it towards his bride, and throwing a kiss with his other hand, he called with loud voice, „Au revoir; in five weeks thou shalt be mine at Vienna!"

It may prove interesting to trace the lives of the sisters and brothers of the late Empress, other than the eldest, of whom I have just spoken. The next in age, Princess Maria Sophia, is the ex-Queen of the Two Sicilies; she married the Crown Prince of Naples, afterwards

Francis II., in 1859, and greatly distinguished herself by her bravery and intrepidity during the siege of Gaeta by the Garibaldian and Italian troops.

Princess Matilda Louisa married Prince Louis of Bourbon, Count of Trani, in 1861, who was brother of King Francis II., and has been a widow for the past twelve years, her husband having committed suicide by drowning himself in a fit of temporary insanity. The youngest. Princess Sophie Charlotte, was the betrothed bride of the unfortunate King Ludwig II. of Bavaria, until he suddenly and mysteriously broke off his engagement; she afterwards wedded the Due d'Alençon (in 1868), and was one of the victims of the memorable conflagration at the Charity Bazaar which plunged the French aristocracy into mourning not long ago. There were also three brothers: Duke Ludwig William, who in 1859 renounced his right of succession upon contracting a morganatic marriage with an actress; Duke Charles Theodore, the renowned oculist and philanthropist, and present head of the ducal house of Bavaria, who resides in Tegernsee in Bavaria; and Duke Maximilian, who died in 1893.

I have had occasion to say before that the Princess Elizabeth preferred roaming through the woods and forests to sitting at a desk to study, but she nevertheless displayed remarkable talent as a student of natural science, geography, drawing, painting, and music, and excelled in the practice of many physical exercises, particularly horsemanship and swimming. She was also all her life a great pedestrian.

CHAPTER II.

THE EMPRESS ELIZABETH.

On the 24th of April, 1854, the Princess Elizabeth of Bavaria became Empress of Austria, the wife of the proudest of all monarchs of Europe, - the Apostolic King of Hungary; King of Bohemia, Dalmatia, Croatia, Slavonia, Galicia, Lodomeria, Illyria, and Jerusalem; a Duke, Prince, or Lord of a hundred other places, and the possessor of more titles than any other sovereign; a man through whose veins flows the blood of all the great reigning families, Bourbon, Plantagenet, and Stuart, as well as that of a hundred Roman Emperors.

The imperial bride arrived at Schönbrunn from Linz in Upper Austria, whence she had taken a steamer, which brought her down the beautiful blue Danube. She landed on Saturday at Nussdorf, near Vienna, where she was met by the Emperor in person.

The solemnisation of the imperial nuptials took place in the Court Church of St. Augustine by the Cardinal Prince Archbishop of Vienna, and the greatest enthusiasm prevailed amongst the populace. The girl bride won the hearts of all; and the greater was the love borne for her when it became known that she had begged of the Emperor, as the first favour to be granted to the wife, the release of the political prisoners, three hundred and fifty-six of whom received pardon. All criminal suits in Galicia for treason were quashed, and similar suits for offences against His Majesty were erased entirely after the ist of May. According to an ancient custom, the bride drove in great state from the Theresianum, where she had arrived early in the morning, to the imperial castle, and was received by a most brilliant assembly, gathered together to do honour to their future Queen. The pageant moved over a new stone bridge, which was named after her the „Elizabeth Bridge." By a strange coincidence this bridge was demolished this year (1898), and so has ceased to exist in the same year as she who had given it her name. The bride wore a pale pink satin dress, beautifully embroidered with silver and adorned with white roses, a white lace shawl, and a most brilliant diamond tiara, which was only partly visible under a wreath of white and red roses. The pomp of the ceremony surpassed anything seen during this century, and the banquet which followed was one of the most magnificent functions recorded in the annals of our times. The wedding took place at 6.30 p.m. The scene was brilliant in the extreme, - the white, red, and blue uniforms of the generals; the gorgeous national costumes of the Hungarian and Polish nobles; the exquisite dresses of the ladies; interspersed with the thickly gold-embroidered costumes of the Privy Councillors, Ministers, and Chamberlains; the scarlet of the Cardinals, and violet of the Bishops; the various, rich, and even fantastic apparel of the Ambassadors and Ministers, combined to form a fairy-like picture of overwhelming grandeur. There were present more than seventy archbishops and bishops, all bedecked with the splendid garments of cloth of gold which are on such occasions used in the Roman ceremonial.

At the entry of the bridal couple the Cardinal Archbishop offered them the holy water, with which they crossed themselves, afterwards taking their places under a rich canopy of gold and velvet. The service lasted about half an hour, after which the thunder of cannon announced to the people that the Princess Elizabeth had become Empress of Austria.

The Emperor and Empress moved now into the Throne Room of the Palace (the Church of St. Augustine adjoins the castle), where the former introduced to the Empress the renowned and venerable Field-Marshal Count Radetzky, Prince Windischgrätz, and the great Croatian hero Jelacic, these three being at the time the greatest in the Empire. Afterwards the Empress received the Ambassadors and Ministers and their wives, generals and high officials, officers and deputations from the various provinces.

After their marriage their Imperial Majesties travelled through Hungary and the Austrian Crown lands, the tour proving a never-ending triumphal procession.

It was reported at the time, and not without truth, that the enthusiastic receptions accorded to her, at least in Vienna, were far more a personal compliment to the young Empress than an expression of loyalty; in fact, the aristocracy of Austria thought that a Princess from a collateral branch of the Bavarian house was not good enough for the Emperor, and they did not disguise their feelings. The arrogant nobles of Vienna actually formed a clique against her, with the natural result that the young couple reserved their smiles and cordial greetings for Buda-Pesth, the second city in the realm, where, in direct contrast to the coolness of the patrician circles in Vienna, the young Princess was literally worshipped.

Soon after Francis Joseph and Elizabeth had been united in matrimony, and when the youthful beauty and affability of the Empress had overcome the adverse feeling entertained by some against her, she was acknowledged to be not only the most beautiful woman but also the most popular queen in Europe; she had a noble bearing, a most fascinating and charming face, encircled by glossy chestnut hair of extraordinary length and thickness, and in addition to rare personal charms she had also great mental gifts, which impressed every one who came in contact with her.

Like her husband's great-aunt, Marie Antoinette, Queen of France, the Empress refused to comply with the strict rules of etiquette. Some of the women of the bed-chamber who were on duty at that time remember to this day what sensations the young Empress created because she would insist on wearing her boots g month or longer, instead of stretching a new pair every day for those who thought that they had a right to them; for according to the ancient customs of the Court the Empress could wear a pair of boots but once.

These said demure creatures of the then most buckram Court of Europe were positively shocked at the indifference to all established rules which the young sovereign displayed.

At the first State dinner, contrary to all custom, she took off her gloves. An elderly Court lady remarked quietly upon it to the young Empress. „Why not," she asked. „Because it is a deviation from the rules," was the answer. „Then let the deviation henceforth be the rule," was the retort; and not that deviation only, but many more, henceforth became the rule, because the new Empress was not an ordinary Princess - she was clever and accomplished in the highest degree, and her will was law: she knew her position.

There was never any doubt that the Empress had no love for the life of state and ceremonial which she had to lead when at home. This was often trying to the patient and loving husband, and sometimes it was supposed that their relations were strained; but innumerable instances prove beyond all doubt that it was not so; and the rumours which some thirty years ago made their appearance from time to time, to the effect that there existed a serious misunderstanding on account of some adventure of the Emperor's, are also discredited by those who ought to know. There is very little if any truth in the tales made up and spread by gossip-mongers, who unfortunately are here and everywhere, and to whom no man or woman is sacred. It will be difficult to believe these stories in the face of the open exhibition of mutual affection displayed on so many occasions by the imperial couple.

Life at the Court of the Habsburgs did not at first offer to the simple-minded Elizabeth the unalloyed happiness she had expected to find at the side of a husband whose love she sincerely reciprocated. I have already mentioned how she came to disagreements with her ladies-in-waiting and Court officials. She created quite a consternation amongst them when she flatly refused to partake of the luncheon consisting of various dainty dishes prepared in the imperial kitchen, and ordered instead some Frankfort sausages and a glass of lager beer, the fare to which she was accustomed. There were many subjects of contention between the imperial bride and the old-fashioned duennas of the Court. It often became necessary for the Emperor to interfere on behalf of his young spouse, and he permitted her to introduce new forms and to lighten the stern rigour of the existing regime. So it came to pass that soon a different tone prevailed in Court circles; and in spite of the venerable mother of the young Emperor, who up to now had been the real mistress of the royal palace, and who opposed any relaxation, and in spite of all the powerful rule of the Jesuits, the Court of Vienna became gay and lively.

Through her influence over her husband the Empress not only caused reforms in their own home, but she also prevailed upon him to greatly alleviate the sad position of prisoners and soldiers who had merited punishment. Chains and corporal punishment were done away with, especially the brutal castigation of soldiers, called „Gassenlaufen,"[1] against which she set her face, and the abolishment of which she demanded, and it was readily granted by her loving spouse as a wedding present. Then, too, the treatment of the poor in the hospitals was strictly investigated, and vast improvements made in that quarter, as a consequence of the interference of Her Majesty on behalf of the suffering poor.

However much Court ceremonies and festivities may have been uncongenial to the Empress, she nevertheless played her part in them for over thirty years with admirable dignity and grace. She moved freely amongst the people, drove in the Prater, the public park of Vienna, and showed herself continually at theatres, the opera, and open-air concerts. It was only the tragic death of her only son, in 1889, which shattered her health and crushed her lofty spirit, that caused her to withdraw from public life, forego all customary exercises, and retire into comparative seclusion, from which she emerged for the first time in 1896 for a few days, on the occasion of the visit paid to Vienna by the young Czar and Czarina of Russia. But even at the great banquet given in honour of the young Russian couple she appeared in deep mourning, affording an especially sad picture amidst the vivid colouring of her surroundings.

During the seven years following her marriage, in the course of which two daughters and a son were born, the conjugal happiness of the Empress Elizabeth would have been complete but for the unpopularity which she incurred among the German subjects, and especially the Viennese, through her dislike to State ceremonials and Court entertainments, and her inveterate love of field sports and the exercises of the *manège*. From early morning to her *déjeuner* she

---

[1] The culprit had to walk slowly through a double row of his comrades, and each struck his bare back with a stout birch rod: frequently he went on till he fainted. It was a cruel practice, which was abolished shortly after Elizabeth had become Empress.

spent her time at the imperial riding school, exercising horse after horse, and in the afternoon she could be seen daily in the Park riding on her private roads, generally using three or four horses in succession. So devoted was she to horse exercise that it was reported she learned to ride without a saddle, kneeling on horseback, and even standing, as we sometimes see done in a circus, for which reason she was nicknamed by the Viennese bourgeoisie „The Circus Rider"; and her infrequent public appearances, despite the charm of her extraordinary beauty and grace, were coldly greeted by the populace of the imperial city. This, combined with the behaviour of the nobility at the time of her marriage, brought about a feeling of dislike for Vienna, whose people she considered narrow-minded, and not unnaturally she was prompted to avoid the Austrian capital throughout nearly four decades of her august consort's reign, and to seek more congenial surroundings in her Hungarian residence.

Unfortunately in 1861 an incipient disease of the lungs compelled the young Empress to quit her country and sever herself for many months from her husband and children. She repaired to Madeira, where she remained for some months, and derived great benefit from its mild climate.

In her habits she was always very simple and frugal, and it was no doubt on that account that even in her sixtieth year, and in spite of the many griefs which she had had to endure, she still looked much younger than she really was. Up to the end of her life she kept her graceful but almost too slender figure; and her hair, which was always one of her chief glories, was still most abundant, though streaked with silver threads; her fine complexion was unimpaired, and her wonderfully deep blue eyes were as expressive as of old. When at Ischl, for instance, she would go out sometimes at 5 a.m. Her walking costumes were very smart, and yet business-like; she had a preference for short skirts in the style of a kilt reaching just above the ankles, and a short jacket over a waistcoat, which varied according to the seasons. As a rule she wore a soft felt hat with blackcock's tail or a grouse's foot, fastening a bunch of her favourite Edelweiss as its only trimming; and a good useful stick was always her companion.

At no place, at home or abroad, did she entertain to any great extent. Now and then, however, a few guests would dine with her, when she always made herself most charming. Her dresses were ever in the best of taste. On one occasion, we read, she wore a white velvet dress made with a high Medici collar edged with white feathers, and a corsage cut square in front, while a deep edging of the feathers round the hem was the only trimming; white suede gloves were on her arms, and her only ornament was, strange to say, a dagger, with the handle formed of very large diamonds, passed through her hair.

Her dinners were simple, but excellent; and the wines, of which there was a great profusion, were of the finest, although she herself only partook of a little claret. A great deal of formality was observed in the waiting, pages of different grades carefully drawing fine lines as to whom they served, those whose position permitted them to wait on the Empress of course ignoring all others.

The Court of Austria is perhaps the most strict and severe as regards etiquette in Europe; and however much the Empress might have liked a quiet and retired life, and however much she might have attempted to bring about changes from the monotony and strictness of the old Spanish etiquette which prevailed, she found it impossible to do away with a great deal of form which was almost mediaeval in its severity. In 1882, when illness prevented Her Majesty from indulging in riding exercise, she became a great pedestrian, and her excursions were sometimes both long and dangerous; but the Emperor, although by no means a good walker, was exceptionally attentive to his imperial spouse, and always did his best to keep up with the Empress in her long walks, and never failed to accompany her during her excursions when staying with her.

Very remarkable was the fearlessness and intrepidity of Her Majesty. At the opening of the Trieste Exhibition in the beginning of the eighties, an Italian irredentist[1] threw a bomb at the festive procession, several persons being wounded. The Emperor and Empress and Crown Prince intended a fortnight later going there; but as danger

---

[1] So were called the members of a party agitating for the severance of Trieste from Austria. They frequently employed violence as their means to an end.

was feared, a general desire was expressed for the Empress to remain away.

„If there is any danger of an attack," she replied to her husband, „I shall certainly go; my place is then by your side." And she went to Trieste.

According to a confession made some time afterwards by the man Oberbank, it had been arranged to kill the imperial pair with a couple of bombs at Trieste. Oberbank was afterwards hanged with his associates.

To mention a predilection of the late Empress of Austria, it may be said that she was extremely fond of jewels, especially of emeralds and rubies, of which she had a marvellous collection.

It was extraordinary how far her generosity reached, and it is well known that no official or servant, either high pr low, who had any hand in contributing to the cordiality of the welcome or the convenience of the Empress in any country, failed to receive a recognition, personally when possible, and by deputy when not. In this country it will be remembered that, on the occasion of her visit to Liverpool, each individual official there and elsewhere throughout the railway system had the agreeable surprise of receiving a few days later a present of jewelry, together with a message of praise and thanks for the way in which they had fulfilled their duties. Each of these souvenirs, one of which was shown to me, must have cost a considerable sum of money.

In the autumn of 1868 the Emperor and Empress, animated by the kindest feelings towards the Poles, resolved to visit Galicia; but while suitable preparations were being made for their cordial reception political disturbances arose, and Count Beust insisted upon their Majesties postponing their visit, as it would endanger the Constitution, and consequently the visit was never carried out. The Empress regretted this very much, as she counted amongst her best friends some of the old Polish nobility.

How difficult it must have been at first for the Empress to move in a sphere so antagonistic to her own ideas can easily be imagined. Whitman, in his Realm of the Habsburgs, speaks thus of Austrian society: „Austrian society is very conservative; even millionaires cannot enter it unless they have a pedigree." An American Minister thirty years ago expressed himself in these words on the subject: „If an Austrian should be a Shakespeare, Galileo, Nelson, and Raphael all in one, he could not be admitted into good society in Vienna unless he had the sixteen quarterings of nobility which birth alone could give him." Austrian noblemen never let ancestral homes to strangers, and they never break their pledged word of honour. Neither the Emperor nor any of his family is ever set upon or hunted down and mobbed in the streets of the capital; they can walk alone and unmolested anywhere.

Only one signal failure can we record in the crusade Her Majesty undertook against the various ancient customs which she considered entirely out of date. As a Roman Catholic and a thinking and logical woman she was strongly opposed to duelling, which is very prevalent, particularly in the army. On one occasion, when two young German noblemen of the Roman faith, who served in a Prussian cavalry regiment, and who had refused a challenge and expressed themselves as opposed on principle of religion to the practice, were obliged to quit the Army, they requested through their mother, who was a personal friend of Elizabeth, that she would prevail upon her husband to give them commissions in one of his hussar regiments. The Emperor, who never could resist an appeal from his consort, caused the Minister of War to make out commissions for the two young counts, but on the day on which they presented themselves at their new quarters the whole corps of officers belonging to the regiment to which the two were commissioned sent in their papers, not being willing to serve with men who had refused to comply with the unwritten code of honour observed in Austria. Naturally the War Minister could not spare gallant officers who had shown their prowess on the field of battle, and the commissions were withdrawn from the two opponents to duelling.

It was said that Her Majesty felt her failure very strongly, but her tact was such that it would not allow her to go openly against public opinion. Nevertheless, she always considered duelling a grievous wrong, and often personally tried to interpose where her own acquaintances were concerned.

When Elizabeth was able to entertain and participate in Court functions, she was known as one of the most charming and affable hostesses, trying her best to make every one feel at home, and herself dancing at and enjoying the balls and *fêtes*. To give a typical picture of an Austrian Court ball, I may briefly describe one which took place only a year ago at the Hofburg in Vienna.

The Emperor entered in Ulan uniform, and was preceded by the Grand Chamberlain, Prince Rudolf Liechtenstein, walking backwards. The Emperor had on his arm the Duchess of Cumberland, magnificently dressed in white and yellow brocade, covered with silver filigree embroidery, and with bunches of violets scattered about the dress and train, which were edged with white marabout feathers. She wore on her head a coronet of leaves and roses, in diamonds. Her daughter, the Princess Marie Louise (who made her *début* at the first State ball), was in pink tulle trimmed with garlands of roses, and wore some exquisite ropes of pink pearls as ornaments.

The Archduchess Stephanie, who is considered one of the best-dressed women in Europe, had a lovely ball dress of dead white satin, covered with a trellis-work of silver and diamonds, and round the bodice was an edging of diamonds on white velvet, and a loosely tied bunch of pink and red roses. In her hair she wore a flat diadem of diamonds, and round her throat a collar of immense diamonds and a necklace of pigeon's-blood rubies. Her Imperial Highness was the most striking-looking woman in the room.

The jewels of some of the wives of the great Hungarian nobles were positively unsurpassable. Countess Esterhazy-Stockau wore a superb castellated crown of enormous diamonds in the mode of the Empire, and her neck and shoulders were literally a plastron of jewels; Princess Montenuovo, the wife of the second Lord High Steward, wore wonderful emeralds; and among the few English present was Lady Rumbold in black. The effect of the magnificent uniforms and marvellous jewels helped to make it an almost unprecedented sight. The commands for the ball were for half-past eight, supper was at eleven, and the whole affair was over by twelve o'clock.

As might be expected, there is an enormous amount of pomp accompanying such balls as the one just described; but perhaps there is even more splendour displayed in religious ceremonies; and the Empress, before her great bereavement in 1889, was foremost in setting the example of attending to religious duties and functions. The grandest spectacle is offered by the yearly procession of Corpus Christi, which wends its way through some of the principal streets of Vienna. The Empress, with the Emperor, followed the Host, which is carried by the Cardinal Archbishop, in jewelled mitre and cope, richly embroidered: the Archbishop walks solemnly under a canopy of purple and gold, and is assisted by a throng of bishops and priests: round them walk representatives of the noblest families of the realm, high officials, knights of the various orders in glittering uniforms, those of St. John and Malta in their long white mantles adorned with a cardinal Maltese cross; Hungarian magnates, Polish princes and counts, in their picturesque national costumes of satin, velvet, and furs, covered with glittering gems of great value; the Hungarian gardes du corps with their leopard-skin mantles, squadrons of cavalry and battalions of infantry.

The Empress on such occasions used to be surrounded by all the Archduchesses, and her devotions were indeed sincere. Another religious ceremony in which she participated was the washing of the feet of twelve poor old women on Good Friday. This seems to be a very ancient ceremony. At the Austrian Court twelve old men and twelve old women from the workhouse are selected, and dressed in the garb of ancient pilgrims, brought to the royal residence, where, in the midst of the greatest pomp, and in the presence of Ministers and Generals, proud Privy Councillors and Chamberlains, officers and pages, accompanied by the bodyguards, the Emperor and Empress with their own hands washed the feet of the respective twelve paupers. This is done to show their humility, as did a Teacher of ethics nineteen hundred years ago in Jerusalem.

As a mother Her Majesty the Empress was always in her element. The birth of a son and two daughters during the first few years of their married life had made the imperial pair the happiest in Europe, so far as their domestic affairs were concerned. During many years

CROWN PRINCE RUDOLF.

ARCHDUCHESS GISELA.

the Empress spent a large amount of her time either in the nursery of her beloved children or in places where poverty and misery could be alleviated. Her most joyful days were those which she spent with her children in solitude at some mountain castle or in some forest villa. She was generally present during the lesson time, and when unable to be so she never missed hearing a full report of the results of their day's teaching. She was particular, too, that the best understanding should exist between teacher and pupil, and although she was most strict in her demands of obedience she was never over-severe, and certainly never unjust; she loved to see her children attach themselves with grateful affection to those who were placed over them, and this feeling was nurtured to such an extent that up to the last the greatest friendship existed between teacher and pupils.

As we have already remarked, besides her idolised only son, the late Empress had two daughters. The elder, the Archduchess Gisela, married, when she was seventeen, Prince Leopold of Bavaria, and has two sons and two daughters; she commemorated this year (1898) her silver wedding. The younger of Her Majesty's daughters, the Archduchess Marie Valerie, who was born, to the joy of the Hungarian people, at Gödölö, on their soil, and educated by a Hungarian, Bishop Ronay, was married eight years ago to the Archduke Francis Salvator of Austria; she has one daughter and four sons.

ARCHDUCHESS MARIE VALERIE.

The Empress of Austria, after her son's death, never saw much of the Archduke Francis Ferdinand, who replaced him as heir to the throne, and who is at present unmarried. It was not from dislike to the young man, who is handsome, tall, fair, and attractive, although unfortunately he possesses very indifferent health, but from a bereaved mother's very natural distaste to seeing any one in her son's place. When the young Archduke was threatened with consumption and his life was almost despaired of, the Empress visited him, and was much touched by his condition.

During the early years of the Empress's married life occurred the disasters which deprived Austria of her most treasured possessions; they did not, however, after the first moment, disturb the conjugal felicity of the Emperor and Empress, but no doubt it was these disasters which caused the Empress to abhor politics. Her husband was her hero, a knight of the days of the Crusades, and gladly would she has seen him lead his armies to battle in person; she was persuaded that then the great reverses which had very frequently attended the Austrian arms could not have taken place. She was proud, as well she might be, of her young consort's splendid courage and his proficiency in all martial exercises, of his power of attaching men to his person, and of his great strategic ability; and when the constitutional era arrived she was wounded deeply to feel that he must sink his brilliant personality, and merely play the part of an ordinary constitutional sovereign - to be an autocrat had been her ideal. Her chagrin and grief found a willing echo in the Emperor's own heart, and there was danger for a time that their private life would be shadowed by these public disasters. Elizabeth, who, with all her eccentricity and singularity, was possessed of very great common sense, had foreseen this contingency and prepared for it. She had resolved that her role should be to make her husband, from the moment he entered her presence, forget the cares and trials of his exalted position, and occupy his mind with a fresh series of ideas, that would not only afford him relaxation, but send him back reinvigorated to his labours, for the advantage of all concerned; and it was in consequence of his wife's love and wise actions that the Emperor has been able to preserve the vigour and energy of youth, although for half a century he has been one of the most hard-working men in Europe.

In 1879 the Empress celebrated her silver wedding. *Fêtes* were given in Vienna and Buda-Pesth, Her Majesty staying part of the week at the former and part at the latter place. The historical pageant, arranged by the great painter Hans Makart, has become renowned for its magnificence and picturesqueness. The principal event took place on Thursday, the 24th of April, in the new votive Church of St. Saviour, the consecration of which was also performed. This, perhaps the most beautiful modern Gothic structure in Europe, was built by public subscription in memory of the escape of the Emperor from death by the assassin's knife, and was opened for public services on that day. The open-air festivities were marred by the weather, for the day was very wet, and the grand allegorical procession had to be postponed. The then Chancellor and Foreign Minister, Count Andrassy, gave a most brilliant soiree at the Foreign Office. The procession of carriages conveying the guests took two hours to pass: the Emperor himself arrived at half-past ten, and stopped an hour. After the close of the festivities, in which the Empress took the greatest interest, the imperial couple, accompanied by the Archduchess Gisela and Prince Ludwig of Bavaria, the Empress's brother, arrived at Buda-Pesth, and spent a week there during the races. It had been intimated that no official reception was desired - indeed, the day and hour of arrival only became known at noon; yet, moved by one impulse, the populace went out to welcome their King and Queen with a warmth and enthusiasm such as even here have rarely been witnessed.

The last rejoicing in which Her Majesty displayed any great interest was on the occasion of the marriage of the Crown Prince Rudolf. The way in which the royal betrothal was brought about at Brussels is so very out of the ordinary, and shows so well the liberal teaching of the Prince's mother, that I will give it in detail.

The Archduke Rudolf proposed in person to Princess Stephanie of Belgium at an evening party given in his honour at the Chateau de Laëken. Among the amusements provided for their Majesties' guests was a concert in the magnificent conservatory attached to the palace. Matters had been so arranged, that, when the company were conducted from the salon to the winter garden, the Archduke and the Princess were left together tête-à-tête for a few minutes. As soon as they were alone the Crown Prince approached Her Royal Highness with a low and formal obeisance, saying, „Madam, will you take me for a husband?" To which plain question the Princess simply replied, curtseying deeply, „Yes, Your Imperial Highness." „Your Royal Highness's answer makes me supremely happy," observed the Archduke. „And I," rejoined Princess Stephanie, „promise that I will do my duty towards you under all circumstances."

No more was said; but the youthful pair, arm in arm, joined the royal circle in the winter garden; and the Archduke, leading his fair companion up to her father, addressed King Leopold as follows: „Sire, I have, with Your Majesty's permission, begged Princess Stephanie to bestow her hand upon me. It is my happy privilege to inform you that my petition has been granted." „I rejoice, Monseigneur," replied the King, „to greet you as my son-in-law." The Princess embraced her mother, and immediately afterwards the betrothal was announced to the assembled public. The Empress had already in former years suffered from painful ischialgia, which made her sojourn in the South, and especially on the lake side, imperative. Her diet was most frugal, and consisted principally of milk and fruit; but unfortunately under this treatment she became anaemic, and was therefore obliged, upon the advice of the doctors, to change her regimen for a stronger one.

During the last month of her life the state of Her Majesty's health became greatly improved; she no longer suffered from insomnia, had more appetite and became visibly stronger. Before going to Switzerland she spent some months at Nauheim in the Duchy of Hesse, where she had been examined by means of the Röntgen rays, and Dr. Schott, her physician, expressed a confident expectation that Her Majesty's stay would prove beneficial. This anticipation was realised, and the improvement made was so marked that she was about to return to Vienna to participate in the *fêtes* which were to take place in connection with her husband's Jubilee. The Grand Duke of Hesse, who, with the Grand Duchess, had visited Her Majesty more than once at her villa at Nauheim, pleased with the success of her medical attendant. Dr. Schott, conferred upon him the title of Professor. Elizabeth had here also received a visit from the Empress Frederick and the German Emperor and his spouse. I need hardly say that the feelings which prevailed in Vienna during the first years of the married life of the Empress underwent a thorough change, and from the year 1860 she became the beloved and popular mistress of the realm. Deep was the sympathy shown to her in the terrible trials which she underwent during her life. A mayor of Vienna, old Dr. Zelinka, once said to the citizens, „No other lady is like our Empress," and he fully expressed the feeling of the Viennese; she was unique,the noblest, the sweetest, and the kindest woman in the Empire. I cannot end the present chapter in a more appropriate manner than by giving a short description of some of the palaces in which the Empress principally dwelt when in Austria, and where she entertained or assisted her husband in State functions. In a future chapter I shall speak of those palaces which she had built herself, and which were her personal property, and where, especially since 1889, she spent the greater part of her life.

In Vienna she occupied that wing of the imperial residence (the Hofburg, a conglomeration of buildings of enormous extent and varied styles) which is called the Bellaria, and which is the most modern part; her rooms were distinguished by their exquisite tastefulness, and entire absence of all ostentation. For many years she selected Schönbrunn, the suburban residence of the Emperor, for her headquarters. This castle, with its very fine gardens and park, its charming summer pavilion, its lakes and its fountains, is an extremely comfortable house, in spite of its enormous dimensions; it is deservedly called the Austrian Versailles; and an idea of its size will be formed when I mention that it contains one thousand four hundred and forty-one rooms and one hundred and thirty-nine kitchens.

From 1805 to 1809 this beautiful and ancient seat of the Habsburgs was inhabited temporarily by Napoleon I.; and his son, the Duke of Reichstadt, King of Rome, died there in 1832. The gardens are adorned with marble statues by Bayer, representing gods and goddesses of the Greek mythology; and one of the most exquisite works of art is the fountain of Neptune - a fine group of marble statuary by Bayer, Von Hasenauer, and Zacherl; they are most picturesquely posed upon granite rock, and form the base of the fountain, two large and many small water jets being thrown up to various heights.

Not far from Vienna there is another extremely picturesque castle, at present occupied by the Crown Prince's widow, named Laxenburg, which was in former years often the home of the murdered Empress, and where the three elder children were born. The park is very extensive and beautiful, containing some charming ornamental waters, and an old ivy-covered feudal castle, the Franzensburg.

The lovely marine residence of the late Emperor of Mexico has also frequently sheltered the Empress Elizabeth. It is one of the finest palaces belonging to the Habsburgs, and is situated on the Adriatic, near Trieste. The gardens, with their semi-tropical vegetation, defy description, the ever blue sky and sea lending a special charm to this lovely spot. Another of the favourite residences was the imperial villa at Ischl, in the province of Salzburg. It lies in a valley encompassed by high mountains, and is surrounded by most picturesque scenery.

31

The imperial couple were accustomed to spend some months annually at that well-favoured spot, and it may be that their love for it was partly due to the fact that it was here that the Emperor and Empress met for the first time.

CHAPTER III.

THE QUEEN OF HUNGARY.

It was soon after her marriage that Elizabeth accompanied the Emperor to Hungary. The revolution of 1848 and 1849, which had been crushed with such terrible severity, and the most disastrous consequences to the Hungarian people, had fostered a feeling akin to hatred against the young Emperor-King. It was therefore the more remarkable that Her Majesty succeeded so rapidly in winning the hearts of the Magyars. „Veni, vidi, vici" - this was the experience of the monarch's beautiful bride.

QUEEN ELIZABETH OF HUNGARY.

The Hungarians are essentially chivalrous and sentimental; their high sense of nobility, their veneration for womanhood, and their extraordinary love of beauty caused them to forget past grievances and wrongs, and to offer their hearts and souls to the lovely, affable, and sympathetic woman, who, at least by name, was their Queen, and who had come to them with such confidence and love.

Who has not heard of the historical scene at the palace at Buda-Pesth more than a hundred years ago, when their then Queen, the great Empress Marie Theresa, threw herself upon their honour and mercy, when hard pressed by Prussia and other enemies, and abandoned by her allies? With the baby King, Joseph II., in her arms, she made her hysterical appeal to the barbaric but chivalrous magnates of Trans-Leithania. „Moriamur pro regina nostra!" was the cry that resounded through the palace. How willingly the Magyars of today would have repeated these memorable words!

There is not the slightest doubt that it was due in a very great measure to the love the Hungarian people bore for Elizabeth that Beust succeeded in 1867 in cementing the union between the two powerful factions of the Empire, and the Hungarians always preserved a grateful remembrance, bordering on ecstasy, of the part the Empress played at the time of the completion of the union with Home Rule (Ausgleich). Elizabeth showed throughout her lite a great predilection for the Hungarian people - no doubt on account, in some degree, of their characteristic seriousness and love for nature: even their songs and music are permeated by a mystic melancholy which brought them into close touch with Her Majesty's own feelings.

At the Coronation, which took place in Buda-Pesth in 1867, the enthusiasm for their Queen broke out in the most extraordinary ovations: all hearts seemed to go out towards her. She understood them so well; and having early in her married life mastered their language, one of the most difficult in Europe, she was able to converse freely with them in their own tongue. When the Emperor had given his consent, in accordance with the desire of the Magyars, to be crowned with the ancient crown of St. Stephen, a deputation of the Hungarian nation appeared also before the Empress in Vienna, begging her that she too would allow herself to be crowned as the Hungarian Queen. Her answer, which I give in full, was characteristic of her, and gave the greatest satisfaction to the members of the deputation:

„With the greatest happiness I fulfil the wish or the nation which you have laid before me, and which coincides entirely with my own most warm desire, and I bless the Providence that has preserved my life for this great moment. Please convey to your people my most sincere thanks and my most heartfelt greeting."

The part Her Majesty played during the various ceremonies and festivities at the royal palace in Buda-Pesth was such that I feel this work would not be complete without at least giving a full description of the Coronation. The pomp and enthusiasm it is difficult to describe; but this much can be said - the centre of all this ecstasy was the youthful Princess, endowed with radiant beauty, whose happy countenance and sweet smiles seemed to throw a sunny light upon all those who had the privilege of gazing upon her.

I cannot do better than give the report of the Coronation as it appeared in the Illustrated London News of June 1867:

„Francis Joseph I., Emperor of Austria and King of Hungary, succeeded to the sovereignty both of the Empire and of the Kingdom nearly twenty years ago; but the Magyars of Hungary, who struggled in 1849 to free their country from its connection with Austria, when they were crushed by the intervention of Russia, have but lately consented to acknowledge him as their King upon a concession of due guarantees for their constitutional liberties. The ceremonies of his Coronation, which took place on the 8th inst. (June 1867) at Buda and Pesth, the twin cities of the Danube forming the capital of Hungary, were extremely splendid.

„The Emperor and Empress, with their relatives the Archdukes, were lodged in the Castle of Buda, on the height above the suspension bridge connecting Buda and Pesth. Here the Emperor, or rather King, as he is called in Hungary, had received deputations from the House of Magnates and the House of Deputies, with their addresses of loyalty, two days before. At seven in the morning a procession of courtiers, officers of State, noblemen, magnates, and knights, with Count Andrassy, the Prime Minister, escorted His Majesty on horseback, the Empress in a carriage, and the Archdukes, from the royal palace to the Parish Church of Buda, where they were met by the Primate of Hungary, the Archbishop of Gran, with other prelates and clergy.

„Having knelt to receive the crucifix and holy water, their Majesties were led into the chapel, the trumpets and kettledrums sounding. Here the Crown jewels were placed in the hands of the barons of the realm, and in the procession which then moved towards the high altar the crown of St. Stephen was borne by Count Andrassy, as representative of the Palatine. The Ban of Croatia, Baron Sokcevic, carried the globe; and the Judex Curiae, M. Majlath, the sceptre; the Tavernicus, Baron Sennyey, the pyx; the Royal Hungarian Cupbearer, the sword of State; and the Royal Hungarian Lord High Chancellor, the cross.

„The Crown jewels were placed on the high altar, and the Archbishop of Kalocsa commenced the service with the formula of the Church according to the Pontificale Romanum. After several responses in Latin, the Emperor was led to the altar, and, kneeling, took the Coronation Oath. His Majesty then descended to the lowest step before the altar, and lay prostrate at full length on his face during the reading of the Litany, at the conclusion of which His Majesty was conducted behind the altar, where he laid aside his pelisse, kalpak, and sabre, and prepared for the unction.

„Next His Majesty was anointed with holy oil by the Primate. This part of the ceremony excited much interest. As the Primate poured the oil on His Majesty's right arm and between the shoulders he prayed reverently; and when the ceremony was over, the King, rising, went behind the altar (where the superfluous unction was dried), and reappeared after a time, and walked to the foot of the throne, where he knelt down and seemed to pray. While he was thus kneeling, the Lord High Chamberlain and Marshal of the Court and officiating prelates approached with the royal mantle of St. Stephen, and placed it solemnly over his shoulders. This is clearly proved to have been a casula, the work of Gisela, Queen of St. Stephen, made in a.d. 1031, and is regarded with the utmost veneration by all Hungarians. It was a gift to the Church originally, and has undergone some mutilation. When it is out of repair, it must be mended by no other hands than those of the Queen herself.

„The High Mass now began, to the blare of trumpets and the roll of kettledrums. The King, surrounded by his officers of high state, was led to the altar, where he knelt and bowed his head to the Primate, who placed the naked sword of St. Stephen in his hand with the words of the formula. The Primate then received back the sword from the Emperor, put it into the sheath, and fastened the belt round his loins. The King now stood erect, and, turning his face to the people, drew the ancient blade, and with vigorous hand made the steel flash in the light, as he cut first in front, then to the right, and then to the left, according to tradition, and returned the sword to its sheath, while the artillery thundered out a salvo from outside the church.

„After brandishing the sword of St. Stephen, the King once more knelt on the highest step of the altar; and there the Archbishop of Gran, as Prince Primate, and Count Andrassy, representing the Palatine, put the crown of St. Stephen on j his head. The Primate, with his hands on the crown, gave the blessing, and presented His Majesty first with the sceptre in his right and the globe in his left hand. Having done this, the Primate removed the sword of St. Stephen from the King's side, and returned it to the Royal Hungarian Cupbearer; and when that was done the second salvo was fired. The King, surrounded by eleven magnates, was now solemnly conducted to the throne, and took his place on it with much solemnity. The Primate, standing on his right, pronounced the words, ‚Sta et retina a modo locum quam huc usque paterna successione tenuisti haereditani jure tibi a Deo delegatum per auctoritatem omnipotentis Dei.' Count Andrassy made a sign, and at once the whole assembly burst into an ‚Eljen,' which was repeated three times with thrilling effect. The cannon thundered from the Blocksberg; the bells of Buda and Pesth burst into chimes.

„The King was crowned. As crowned he presented his consort to the Primate, and demanded that she might be crowned; and another service commenced, the crown and insignia being laid on the altar. The service for the Queen was similar to that of the King; a crown was put on her head, but the royal crown was only held on her right shoulder for a time, after which it was replaced on the head of the King. At one time the King and Queen lay prostrate on their faces, as His Majesty had done. After the ceremonies were completed, the King and Queen went in procession through the church gates to the garrison church, where all the royal insignia, except the crown, were laid aside, while the King made a number of knights, dubbing them with the sword of St. Stephen.

„The procession, on marching from the church to go from Buda across the river to Pesth, was formed very much as it started; but it was swollen by the banderia of the counties, by the bishops and prelates and mitred abbots, who formed a very fine-looking body of cavalry; and by the bearers of insignia, who took their places on splendid horses. The magnates and noblemen were also mounted, but attended by their footmen and hussars a pied in the most costly and curious liveries.

„After a time a break was made in the procession by the appearance of some Court footman, and a singular horseman in an old faded greenish mantle, with a helmet-shaped cap of metal on his head. This was the King whom they had crowned. He rode a tall and powerful cream-coloured charger, which was restive enough to show his rider's powers to great advantage, and as he passed enthusiastic cheers greeted the monarch from the crowds of his people, rolling like a flood as he went. The procession wound round by the quays and streets till His Majesty came to the square in front of the Parish Church of Buda; here a tribune was erected, three feet high, covered with cloth of gold, at the foot of the monumental column in honour of the Virgin Mary. This was the tribune on which the King took his stand; and there in the presence of the people, raising three fingers of the right hand to heaven and holding aloft a crucifix in his left, with his face to the east, he took the oath amidst three tremendous ‚Eljens,' and salvos and volleys of musketry.

„The procession then returned from the church to the Franz Josef Platz, where an artificial mound had been raised for the last scene of the Coronation Ceremony. At half-past eleven the King of Hungary rode up to the summit of the hill alone. His appearance was hailed with tremendous cheers. He raised the sword and cut towards the east; then he turned towards the west, and cut in that direction again; he wheeled his horse towards the south, and cut again; and the sword cross was completed when he made his sword gleam towards the north. This performance made a very effective scene.

„The King then rode down, and the mob rushed in, and in an instant the square was filled with people shouting ‚Eljen' till the welkin rang.

„Baron, afterwards Count Beust, the Prime Minister of Austria, came in for a share of the applause. „On the return to the palace there was a State banquet, to allow the Court functionaries to perform their duties, while the magnates waited at table. The people were revelling in the meadow close at hand, where six hogsheads of wine and three whole oxen roasted were provided for all comers."

What a noble deed of the royal couple to hand over the Coronation gift of 100,000 ducats for the foundation of a fund for the assistance of widows and orphans of the very soldiers who in 1849 had fought for their liberty against the Emperor Francis Joseph! What a complete reconciliation when we see the foremost person at the Coronation to be Count Julius Andrassy, who had been condemned to death as a traitor in 1849, and had only escaped with his life by precipitate flight from his country!

It was on the occasion of the Coronation that the Hungarian nation presented their Queen with the Castle of Gödölö, situated in charming scenery not far from the capital. It has been frequently maintained by those who are in a position to know best that Elizabeth spent her happiest days at Gödölö: here all pomp and show was dispensed with; here she kept her hunting stud and kennels; here she was entirely her own mistress, unrestrained by Court ceremony, surrounded by her favourite ladies-in-waiting, equerries, and servants; and here she indulged in the life she loved best. The Magyars simply adored and worshipped her. It is certain that she fully returned their affection with a heartiness the sincerity of which was never doubted in the Kingdom of the Five Rivers. She shared their field sports, to which she imparted a prestige and an impulse of unprecedented force; her knowledge of their national history and literature was complete; and she won the love of all, high and low, and the admiration and appreciation of such renowned scientists as Ferencz Pulsky and Vambery.

She counted amongst her most intimate friends many Hungarians, of whom I will only mention Count Julius Andrassy, Abbé Liszt, Count Maylath, and Tiska. The great novelist Moritz Jokai called her his „ideal of a noble woman."

Deak, the greatest of Hungarian patriots of the century, pronounced her „the noblest Hungarian of them all"; and, having refused titles and money as the reward of his services to his country, accepted, instead of honours and wealth, a simple pair of slippers, worked for him by the loving hands of the Queen of Hungary. Before he died she visited him on his sick-bed at the hotel „Queen of England," and after his death she watched and prayed by his coffin, and manifested her sincere grief by the tears she shed as she knelt at the foot of his justly venerated bier.

On this occasion she showed her wonted tact, when, being informed that the recovery of Hungary's Hampden had become very doubtful, she sent one of her equerries to his hotel to ask if she might be allowed to come and visit him; and when he had closed his eyes for the everlasting rest, and as the body lay in the hall of the Royal Academy, which was transformed into a chapel of mourning, a simple Court carriage arrived at the door, and the Empress, dressed in deep mourning, entered. She held in her hand a wreath of laurels, with beautiful camellias and white satin ribbons, inscribed with the words: „Erzsebet Kiralyne Deak Ferencznek" („Queen Elizabeth to Frantz Deak"). A few minutes she stood in contemplation before the coffin, tears rolling down her cheeks; then she placed the wreath upon the bier, and knelt down and prayed. This scene has been immortalised by two of Hungary's greatest painters - Munkacsy and Michael Ziczy. The only time during the Empress's life that she evinced any interest in politics was when she assisted in the reconciliation of the Austrian and Hungarian Governments, It was the absence of Her Majesty - who, overwhelmed by so many disasters, could not be prevailed upon to participate in the festivities of the onethousanth year of Hungarian independence (celebrated in 1896) - which threw a shadow over the large assembly of Hungarian patriots. In spite of the enthusiasm and the great pomp which were displayed at the various ceremonies of the time, the absence of the Queen who was so much loved prevented the occasion from being the success which it would otherwise have been.

In what esteem, ay, reverence, the Hungarians held their Queen was well expressed by the passing of a Bill in the Houses of Parliament, soon after she had lost her life, for perpetuating her name by inserting a record of her life in the archives of the nation and erecting a monument to her memory in the Hungarian capital by voluntary subscriptions.

CHAPTER IV.

THE EMPRESS AS A WOMAN, PHILANTHROPIST, FRIEND, AND MISTRESS.

The influence which the Empress brought to bear upon the vexed question of woman's rights is of great importance, even if we accept the opinions of some who maintain that she was not in favour of inducing women to take too large an interest in politics. But she has doubtless contributed much to the accomplishment of the undeniable fact that womankind has made remarkable progress in the realm during the long reign of her husband, who, as is well known, ever consulted her when questions arose or needed decision in which the fate of women was concerned. The changes in the position of women which took place during the forty-four years in which the Empress shared the throne of Francis Joseph are enormous, especially in the higher circles and the middle classes.

It was ever one of Her Majesty's endeavours to alleviate also the position of the working women, which unfortunately is still such as to need urgent reform. It was upon her initiative that an inquiry was recently made into the conditions under which working women live in Austria, and especially in Vienna. The disclosures resulting therefrom caused Her Majesty the deepest grief, and in a letter written to a noble man who might well be called the Austrian Shaftesbury she begged him to do all in his power to see that a change was speedily made, assuring him at the same time of her most hearty co-operation.

The inquiry was conducted during the spring of 1896 by the Society of Ethical Culture. The state of affairs brought to light was most lamentable; and the Empress, shortly before her death, made the strongest representations to the Home Secretary, in order to induce him to see that the terrible misery existing among the lowest class of women and girls should be changed. „My heart bleeds," she wrote, „when I think of the misery of those poor women and girls, who work like slaves of ancient times, without even being able to earn enough to feed themselves properly. The vessel entrusted by God with the propagation and continuation of mankind should at least be above want - the gratitude of us all demands so much."

We give a few items from the report referred to, in order to show how justified the Empress was in expressing her indignation in the strongest words:

„In box-making the apprentices are compelled to work during many months at wages of one florin (is. id.) a week ... The confectioner's trade shows a great mortality from lung disease, caused by the sugar dust, which is also very injurious to the eyes; the women must often work at a temperature of 148° Fahrenheit. The average age attained by the work-people is thirty-two years. In the flower and feather industries hundreds of young girls are kept in a kind of domestic slavery, and are forced to work sixteen, eighteen, even twenty hours a day for their board, lodging, and a few pence per week. They are miserably fed and packed two or three in one bed, a single room often containing three or four such beds.

„Apprentices usually work three years without any payment. At carnival times the girls sometimes work the whole night; and during several months the time allowed them for sleep is very short. A similar system is found in the glove and bandage trades; the workers - mostly young girls hired from the country districts - are exhausted by overwork, ill lodged, ill fed, and still worse paid. In the embroidery trade there is intense competition, partly caused by the homework of women of the lower middle class. Gold and silk embroidery - very trying to the eyes, especially at night - is largely done by quite young girls, kept as apprentices many years, and paid about two florins a week; a very highly skilled work-woman earns about fifty to sixty kreutzers a day. Liver and lung diseases are very common in this industry.

„The hardest labour performed by women is in brick-making and house-building; in the latter they are obliged to draw carts containing great loads of mortar, to carry heavy mortar buckets up the scaffolds, and to endure cold and heat during a working day of sixteen or seventeen hours, labouring away, true martyrs, up to a motherhood that brings them no joy and allows them no rest ... Besides the trades mentioned, the condition of milliners, washerwomen, shop-girls, and so forth has been investigated; but the examples given will be sufficient to show the want and misery endured by female workers in Austria ... A great number of the women die prematurely, and but a small percentage are able to bear and rear healthy children."

It is to be hoped that for the sake of the sacred memory of the Empress Elizabeth, whose sympathy was so warmly engaged in this matter, steps will betaken without delay to alleviate the fate of these poor innocent creatures. Anyhow, the first step has been taken, for the classes knew that they had a strong protectress in the wife of their sovereign, and her teaching has caused in women an awakening to their true calling, and through this the incipient emancipation from their former thraldom. I am able to pay a reverential tribute to the exalted lady for the noble work she has done in this regard, by setting an example which has exerted the greatest influence throughout the land. It was that most beneficent lady, the youthful Empress Elizabeth, who, shortly after she had taken her place as mistress of the feudal Court in Vienna, broke the fetters which old custom and usage had placed on the gentle sex, the highest and the lowest, and by her example gave an impetus to the agitation which produced the comparatively healthy state of affairs which now exists, at all events in the upper and middle classes.

Without following even partly the movement and its development, I intend to give some instances of what must have been the outcome of this long and beneficent work, and we cannot but rejoice, not only at the bright examples of the women and their Empress in Austria, but also to find that they were fully appreciated by all classes of the Empire. Their influence upon the social state, and not infrequently even upon politics, has been incalculable, for they have taken the lead in many social movements, and by their perseverance, patience, and tact have carried to a successful issue many important plans.

The beginning of the festivities in connection with the Jubilee, which received such a terrible check, the Empress as a Woman took place towards the end of June at Vienna. A great procession and pageant of marksmen and huntsmen, consisting of more than twenty thousand men from all parts of the Empire, with contingents from Bavaria and other German states, moved through the principal streets of the capital; and one could not help being strongly impressed by a particular feature in the procession - namely, the prominent and honoured position given to womankind in a pageant which fifty years ago would certainly have been considered essentially a masculine one. There marched among the marksmen a goodly troop of markswomen, who had won many victories in former shooting matches, and who were enthusiastically cheered by the enormous crowds of sightseers as they passed in their neat uniforms, carrying their rifles on their shoulders. Here could be clearly traced the influence of the Empress-Queen, who had herself devoted much time to athletic exercises and to sports of all kinds that assisted physical development; for she was throughout her life a warm advocate of outdoor pastimes and of healthful recreation.

Among the various waggons which adorned the marksmen's procession, and upon which groups were arranged, one of the finest was the one representing „Austria." On a throne tastefully draped with silks and satins in the Austrian colours, a sword of state in her right hand, and the left resting on a shield of gold emblazoned with the arms of the Empire, sat a youthful dame of great beauty and dignity.

A second waggon carried a bust of the venerable Emperor, surrounded by „Vindobona" (emblematic of Vienna), the Muse of History, the Genius of Peace, and the Goddess of War, all represented by Viennese ladies, guarded by officers of the Viennese Volunteers in the uniform of 1809 to 1866. But especially picturesque was the *cortège* of this festal waggon, which consisted of about sixty ladies in the costume of Old Vienna, accompanied in some cases by their swains. The fact that this part of the procession was the most popular, was cheered more than any other, is a proof that the women of the Empire and their work are duly appreciated.

That woman's political and social position has so much altered, and that there are today the highest schools of learning equally open to both sexes, is no doubt due to the fact that their capabilities have become so evident that any further attempt to suppress them must have proved abortive, and that they not only engage the sympathy of all thinking men, but also the esteem and admiration of the great majority who have hitherto blindly denied even the intellectual equality of women with men.

But I must not overlook the teaching of the highest lady in the land, and it is not too much to say that the late Empress introduced into Austria a perfectly new regime. She was brought up by her parents in simplicity, but with liberal ideas; she was allowed to mix freely with the masses, and in this wise to become acquainted with all conditions of men and women; and the lessons of her girlhood's days were not forgotten when she was called upon to share the throne of a powerful potentate. She was for her time certainly an „advanced" woman.

Her influence upon the Viennese Court was quite extraordinary, and soon the female element became as much a part of the realm to be taken into consideration as the male one. The Emperor, whose love for her was so true and sincere, was happy to assist her in this work; but whether she converted him to her ideas, or whether he had emancipated himself on his own initiative from the old narrow way of the imperial family, it would be difficult to state.

The fact remains that in honouring people the Emperor made no difference on account of sex, and there was at least one high order long existing in Austria which was bestowed on ladies only. Be it granted that the Sternkreutz Order was only given to noble dames; but it was an order of knighthood, and its very existence proved that women's equality with men was recognised at the Court, even at a time when it otherwise deserved to be called the most narrow-minded in Europe.

The part taken in politics during the era of Napoleon III. by the wife of the then Austrian Ambassador in Paris, Princess Paulin Metternich, has become historical, and similar important positions were held by the Countess Taafe and many others. Princess Metternich must be remembered amongst the remarkable women of the century; she is at present engaged in writing her memoirs, which are sure to contain many most interesting incidents of the last eleven years of the Second Empire.

Her friendship with the Empress Elizabeth was very intimate, and it appeared that the two ladies had many objects in common.

Prince Richard presented his credentials as ambassador to Napoleon III. in December 1859; he was then only thirty-one years old, and the Princess twenty-four - the very prime of life for both; she was the daughter of a great Hungarian nobleman, the late Count Sandor, one of the most renowned sportsmen and horsemen in that country, and of whose wonderful feats, achievements, and foolhardy undertakings on horseback Hungary is even now full. Soon after the Princess had established herself in the French capital she became a *persona gratissima* in the Tuileries; her accomplishments were many, her influence great, and as a conversationalist she had no rival; she wielded an enormous power, and history some future day will tell what beneficent use she made of it. It was she who introduced Wagner's music into Paris. Tannhäuser was received absolutely with derision. „And now," the Princess said a short time ago to an ambassador in Vienna, „the Parisians are more Wagnerian than I am myself."

With the fall of Napoleon, Prince and Princess Metternich returned to Vienna, and the Princess's influence upon society was soon felt there. After the death of her husband in 1895 she retired almost entirely from Court life, but re-entered it this year (1898), and her first reappearance was at a most charming charity *fête* held in the Belvedere Gardens in Vienna, under the patronage of Her Majesty and the Archduchesses. The Empress, although absent, took the warmest interest in the philanthropic undertaking. It was an al-fresco arrangement, and tents of various colours, ten of each shade, ran down the centre avenue; the articles sold in each tent were of the same colour, and the dresses of the ladies matched. Princess Metternich herself presided at one of the violet tents, and was in lilac silk trimmed with old point de Venice; Countess Beckers wore violet and white checked silk, and a bonnet trimmed with purple and white hyacinths; Princess Montenuovo had a blue stall, and wore corn-flower muslin trimmed with quantities of Valenciennes lace; Countess Wydenbruck, who had as assistant Miss Clemens (Mark Twain's daughter), was in green silk, and wore a hat with wild roses. The rose-coloured tents had keepers in all shades of pink and crimson, Princess Schwartzenberg being in deep pink and wearing a toque of carnations. All these ladies had been honoured by the late Empress's friendship. There was a novelty in the shape of a market-place, where noble ladies sat under huge mushroom umbrellas of different gay colours, and sold country produce, which included splendid grapes, fine peaches, and juicy nectarines.

I have described this fair more in detail because it must stand as a type for many similar *fêtes* and because I wish to show as an undisputed fact that ladies under the leadership of Elizabeth or her deputy raised almost all the funds for the extensive charitable work in Austria. Their indefatigable energies and their resources seem to come to no end.

As hostesses Viennese ladies rank very high. It was the cause of the greatest regret when the late Empress entirely retired from Court life after the death of her much-beloved son the Crown Prince; but the spirit which she had introduced still remained, and her place was most fitly filled by either the Archduchess Marie Theresa (before she became a widow) or the Archduchess Otto, the Crown Prince's widow rarely caring to be conspicuous at Court festivities. However, the great hostess of today is the Archduchess Isabel, the wife of the Archduke Frederick, who is the possessor of immense wealth and of a splendid palace well situated for entertainments upon a large scale. Her balls, next to the Court balls, are the most brilliant and exclusive, only imperial and royal personages, the members of the highest aristocracy, diplomats, and those holding high positions in the military and civil services having the entree to them. Princess Isabel is the mother of seven daughters, and one son (born quite recently), and is much liked in society; her husband is an able and popular soldier; and it may be said that the Empress always showed a very great liking for this imperial couple. I may mention here also that there is not a more popular lady in Viennese society than the wife of the British Ambassador, and the balls at the Embassy are counted among the best during the season; they were some of the few which in former days were honoured by Her Majesty's presence.

47

It would be quite impossible to give even an approximate list of the ladies of the gay world, of the *haute finance,* etc., who are of renown as hostesses in that city, and as difficult would it be to describe the wholesome change which has taken place during the last forty years in the entertainments themselves. The formerly strictly observed ceremonial and etiquette have given place to a nonchalance and freedom introduced at Court by the Empress when a bride, which make the *fêtes* of today really affairs of pleasure.

Like our own country, Austria has, during the two or three last decades, produced some women renowned as novelists, poetesses, and actresses, who have been highly honoured and appreciated, and whose social position has become equal to any: we will name from the many only Madame Wolter, who married Count O'Sullivan, and Fräulein von Hohenfels, both of whom could boast not only of the esteem but also of the friendship of their imperial mistress. Many women have attained to a high degree in art, both in painting and in sculpture, and have been distinguished by the Emperor.

If we look into the lower spheres of society, we cannot help finding also here an evident change for the better. The helpmate of the labouring man has become his counsellor, and the idea that there must be a master and a slave in the household has disappeared. Husband and wife we find today on equal terms, each attending to his or her duties, and especially amongst the farmers,where we may frequently see that the woman occupies the superior position in the household.

In order to perpetuate the work of his beloved consort, Francis Joseph has established a new order for women, called the Elizabeth Order, and the rescript which was issued with the establishment of this decoration shows how completely Francis Joseph understood and appreciated the influence which his wife had brought to bear upon the female portion of his Empire.

The Emperor wrote thus to the Minister of the imperial house, Count Golukowsky: „Bowed down by the deepest grief through the great loss which has come over my house and my peoples by the sudden death of my most beloved wife, the Empress and Queen Elizabeth, in order to create a perpetual memorial to the departed, I have decided to found an order for women, which I have named in memory of her whom I have so truly loved, and for whom I grieve so deeply, the Elizabeth Order."

And here follow the words to which I wish particularly to call the attention of my readers. The Emperor continues:

„The late Empress had been all through her life anxious to do good, and to alleviate the suffering of her neighbours; and therefore this new-founded order shall have the purpose of rewarding women and girls in every condition and in every sphere of life or profession for deeds of humanity or philanthropy, thus following the example set by the illustrious dead."

The first to receive this order was Countess Sztaray, who accompanied the late Empress when she was murdered by the dastardly hand of Lucheni.

The sympathetic heart of the royal victim of an anarchist had ever been looking round to see where she might bring consolation and alleviation of suffering. With what compassion she entered the villa of the ex-Empress Eugenie at Cap Martin, embracing the sufferer warmly and showing through that act that the change of position made no difference in her own feelings! Never will it be forgotten with what tender love she attended the ex-Empress Charlotte of Mexico when the terrible death of her husband had darkened her intellect, and frequently would she visit the poor wife of the murdered Maximilian, who suffers mentally and lives a secluded life at Laëken, near Brussels in Belgium.

Whenever the late Empress was needed at a place of misery, there, like a good fairy, she appeared, bringing help to the sick and poor. When during the wars the wounded soldiers arrived by rail at the hospitals in Vienna, she herself received them at the station, visited them day and night at the hospitals, consoling, assuring, alleviating. One of her noble deeds which has become known out of the many she was ever doing shows better than words the kindness of her heart. It was a young trooper, whose wounds were of such a nature that his recovery became almost an impossibility; the Empress stood at his bedside, asking him if she could do anything for him, when he

VILLA OF THE EX-EMPRESS EUGENIE AT CAP MARTIN.

humbly informed her that his great wish was that a letter should be written to his mother, sister, and sweetheart, who were many miles away in Trans-Leithania, and whom he felt he would never see again. The imperial visitor promised that his desire should be carried into effect, and immediately on her return home she dispatched one of her equerries down to the little Carpathian village with orders to bring immediately the relatives of this soldier to Vienna, and a few days afterwards she personally had the pleasure of leading the poor old mother and the two younger women to the bedside of the cavalry-man. Who could describe the pleasure and happiness which existed for some hours at that sad bedside? But a reward which was not expected came to Her Majesty: through the nursing of his loving relatives death was warded off, and in spite of the assertions of the doctor that his life could not be saved the young soldier recovered, and, liberally endowed by Her Majesty, was able within a year to be married to the choice of his heart, who had assisted in nursing him back from death's door.

But it was not only the wounded to whom the Empress gave sympathy. Frequently she spent hours at the bedside of sufferers in the hospitals in Austria and Hungary, lightening their heavy burdens by her charming conversation and her compassionate words, and more than once were the physicians obliged to request the exalted visitor to think of her own health and seek much-needed rest.

In every aspect of her varied character she was admirable, in none more so than in her sympathy with the weak and suffering and her strict love of justice. Her sphere of benevolence was unlimited; at home or abroad her purse was ever open to those who needed assistance. She was a bountiful benefactress to the churches and charities in Paris, as in every place where she sojourned.

Can it be wondered at, that, with such a woman at the head of society, the tone of it should be the best? The Emperor, who so fully entered into the new spirit which the Empress had introduced, was always willing to recognise the merits of women in as full a measure as those of men, and on various occasions he showed pointedly his regard for the gentler sex. Some years ago he attended a Tyrolese rifle meeting at Innsbruck, and, joining in the spirit of the thing, not only distinguished the pretty peasant girl who was deputed to hand the Emperor flowers and his mug of wine by pressing a kiss upon her brow, but caused her to journey especially to Vienna to be received in private audience by the Empress, who presented her with a diamond cross as a souvenir.

In the more intimate circle of the Emperor's family the prevailing tone is a most charming one; the Archduchesses have laid aside all their stiffness of former years, and appear as women among women, and the Empress herself always advocated marriages where love should play a more important part than *convenance*. Her own youngest daughter was married to the choice of her heart, and no considerations were allowed to stand in her way. Even in cases of *mésalliances* the Empress had always shown great kindness and friendliness to the ladies who have been chosen as spouses by her relations, and never allowed them to feel in any way their inferiority of birth.

It was often said that no one could be a truer and more sincere friend than the Empress Elizabeth, and those to whom she allowed the privilege of joining the circle of her friends were soon convinced of her unselfishness, true kindness, and noble nature. The ladies of her Court worshipped her; the gentlemen would willingly, one and all, have laid down their lives for their imperial mistress. Her servants, of whom a great many were English and Irish, showed always the greatest devotion to her, and to be in her personal service was considered one of the most coveted of positions.

One of the privileges of the Empress of Austria is the nomination of „Palast Damen" (ladies of the palace), a much-coveted dignity, as it gives the free entree to the more intime Court circle, and would correspond perhaps with our extra or honorary ladies-in-waiting. Elizabeth was most happy in her selections, but even here she could not free herself entirely from her love for the beautiful, and it was often stated by connoisseurs that the bevy of lovely young women and girls with whom she liked to surround herself afforded a most charming picture. Many of those whom she especially honoured with her friendship are amongst the past and present beauties of the Empire. Some of our portraits will speak for themselves, and confirm what can only be inadequately described.

The Princess Montenuovo and the Countesses Pototzka, Wydenbruck, Josephine Kinsky, and Haas-Wächter are a few of the galaxy.

The spirit of chivalry which Her Majesty implanted in Austrian society has been marvelous; and one of the first instances - quite a typical one -is the deed of a woman, the sister-in-law of the Empress, the Archduchess Marie Theresa, who actually put to shame the stronger sex in an emergency. When staying at her country residence, a fire broke out in a village in the neighbourhood; whereupon she instantly ordered her carriage, and drove to the scene of the conflagration; there she learnt that in one of the rooms of the house a little child was imprisoned; seeing the men standing around reluctant to risk their lives, she dashed up the burning staircase before anybody had time to prevent her, returning in, a few moments with the child practically unhurt in her arms. The brave Princess's hair was scorched and burnt, and her hands were badly injured, but she refused to receive medical aid until the doctor had satisfied her that the little one was unhurt.

Although herself overwhelmed by a burden of misfortunes, Elizabeth never seemed happier than when able to act the part of the consoling angel; and her friendship, love, and almost reverence for those who had passed through distress and bitter woe were unspeakably strong and heartfelt; it was for this reason that she harboured in her heart so much devotion and esteem for the venerable ex-Queen of Hanover, the oldest royal lady now living, who, since her late husband lost his throne, has made her home in the Austrian Empire.

Naturally all the great philanthropic and charitable institutions in Austria and Hungary, and even some in foreign countries, were under the protection of the Empress; and in 1875, at the one-hundredth year of its existence, the Institute for the Free Education of Officer's Daughters received her special attention. She sent a donation of ten thousand florins, and made a strong appeal to the public on behalf of the institution; and, to her great pleasure, this resulted in an addition to its funds of more than half a million florins. In a similar way she helped the Establishment for the Care of Daughters of Poor Civil Servants.

In 1878, after the occupation by Austria of Bosnia and Herzegovina, during which so many soldiers lost their lives, she perceived the necessity for the establishment of a regular fund for the assistance of those who were wounded or ill. In the letter written by her own hand to the Prime Minister, she proposed the formation of the Patriotic Women's Union for the purpose of assisting soldiers in poor circumstances, and of nursing the sick and wounded. This fund is now well established, and the members, who reside in all parts of the vast Empire, are intimately united in carrying out the benevolent intentions of the „mother of the country."

In closing this chapter I cannot forego repeating the conviction, that, however nobly the murdered Empress may stand out as the mistress of a great Court, as the consort of a powerful Emperor, as mother, student, philanthropist, as a woman among women, her memory must shine with a yet greater lustre.

Her husband, the Emperor himself, paid her, perhaps, the highest compliment, when, in addressing an assembly of his loyal Hungarians some time ago, he spoke these memorable words: „Without her I could never have done the work that God has given me to do."

CHAPTER V.

THE EMPRESS AS A STUDENT AND READER.

So lofty a character as that of the Empress Elizabeth must needs show a great leaning towards poetry, music, and art. That she found great consolation and forgetfulness of uncongenial realities whenever she could give herself up entirely to the pathos and poesy of her favourite writers has been frequently proved, and studies of the sublime and noble rendered her oblivious of the prose of every-day life.

The melancholy music of the lyre of Heinrich Heine had a soothing influence upon her, and it is no doubt for that reason that she loved him so dearly. We are able to give in translation the poems she especially admired, and which are marked in her volumes, and show traces of their frequent perusal, even to the distinct marks of tears which had fallen on the pages as they were read.

> *You little hand lay on my heart, dearest dear!*
> *Do you in that small room a great knocking hear?*
> *There a carpenter dwells, hard and cunning is he,*
> *Who is nailing together a coffin for me.*
>
> *Such hammering and knocking, by night and by day!*
> *Long since it has driven my sleep quite away.*
> *Be quick now, Master Carpenter, please!*
> *So that I soon may sleep at ease!*

* * *

> *Thy face so sweet and fair doth seem;*
> *Of late I saw it, but in dream:*
> *So mild in its angelic grace.*
> *But pale, with sorrow pale, thy face.*

Only the lips like rosebuds blow,
But, kissed by death, soon blanched grow;
To heaven withdrawn, from whence it came;
Of holy eyes the dying flame.

* * *

There stands a fir tree lonely
On a naked Norland height;
He sleeps - ice and snow enfold him
Beneath a coverlet white.

* * *

He dreams there of a palm tree
In the Morning-land afar,
Lonely in silent sorrow
On a bare cliff's burning scaur.

* * *

Death is the cool and quiet night,
And life the weary, sultry day;
The darkness falls - I sleep away
The toils and troubles of the light.

Her veneration for the German bard took also a practical form. She never visited Paris without making a pilgrimage to his grave in the Montmartre Cemetery.

She has even left the record of one of these visits to the burial-place of her favourite author in some verses, noting in these compositions that before reaching „God's acre" she went to the church of Notre Dame des Victoires, in order to pray for the repose of the soul of her beloved poet. She also gave instructions to have the grave taken care of and flowers placed upon it from time to time.

The Empress was an enthusiast for all that was English, and her studies of English literature were continuous. She was a devoted Shakespearian scholar, and her own commentator; she translated his Tempest y Hamlet y King Lear and parts of others of his immortal

55

plays into modern Greek. Next in favour was Byron and after him Longfellow.

Of prose-writers she especially admired George Eliot and Lord Byron, but she read also with great interest the novels of Mrs. Humphry Ward, and was much impressed by Florence Marryat's „The Blood of the Vampire." She is also reported to have been particularly struck with the imaginative power of Marie Corelli's writings, and only this year (1898) she sent her a letter assuring her that her books had given her many hours of happiness and rest. The Empress regretted that the novelist should have vented her own private grievances against the critics, and considered that in those passages Marie Corelli had been guilty of a literary indiscretion which somewhat marred the beauty of the story.

It was a strange coincidence that the last English novel the Empress read with her permanent English reader, Mr. Barker, should have been Marion Crawford's „Corleone," which deals with the organisation of the Maffia in Sicily. She was strongly moved by the horrors of the work. Mr. Barker states that he selected „Corleone" in order to make the Empress familiar with the murderous machinations of bloodthirsty wretches, hoping it might lead to her taking more care of her personal safety.

It will throw some light upon the characteristics of the Empress Elizabeth, if we show how it came about that she engaged Mr. Barker as her reader.

The gentleman in question seems a veritable personage out of the Orient of one's travels, combined with the living plastic of a Greek „study" in modern garb.

We cannot do better than report verbatim the interview the correspondent of the Pall Mall Gazette had with Mr. Barker shortly after the assassination of his imperial mistress:

„Mr. Barker himself must have noticed my curiosity, and proceeded to explain.

„I am an Englishman, although you perhaps wonder how that can be. Well, my father was an Englishman and my mother an Oriental. My grandfather was British Consul in Egypt. How did I become acquainted with the Empress? Oh, that was at Alexandria in 1891 - a very interesting episode. I was lying ill from malaria, caught at Corfu, when my favourite brother and intimate friend - you smile at that expression, but surely a relative is not necessarily a friend! - rushed in one day with the intelligence that the Empress was at Cairo. „Frederick!" he said, „write a poem about her palace at Corfu and dedicate it to her." I laughed at the idea. I believe I said in my impatience, „Confound the Empress!" But, anyhow, I allowed myself to be persuaded, and a few months later I received an invitation to visit her on board the Miramare, lying in Alexandria Harbour.

Her Majesty was sitting alone on deck. She thanked me in that sweet manner that was hers for the poem, and put questions to me in various languages. Half an hour afterwards the Miramare sailed.

„ ,The gentleman who writes Greek so well,' as she described me, did not see her again until the spring of 1892, when she asked me if I would join her for a couple of months on a trip. Those two months were extended to thirteen, and in 1897 I was appointed her permanent reader. And now the end has come - the end, *per Dio,* to a life that was an earthly paradise. The world will surely never see her like again.'

„ ,You were very much with the Empress, I believe?',, ,Yes, sometimes as much as twelve hours a day. You see I am a linguist, and if her Majesty was not speaking Hungarian with Countess Sztaray, she was chatting Greek, Italian, French, or English with me.' "

Mr. Barker states that the late Empress spoke English better than German. „When she was feeling well, we would start reading at about half-past eight o'clock. Sometimes I would sit and sing to her some of my Greek pastorals and lyrics on the guitar. She was herself a poetess - I might say a demi-goddess." With these words Mr. Barker terminated his interview with the *Pall Mall Gazette* correspondent.

I may mention here that the Empress found also much pleasure in the Irish tales of Charles Lever, whose personal acquaintance she had made during the time the novelist was British Consul in Trieste.

The Empress did not neglect French authors, past and present, as she read the works of Jean Jacques Rousseau, and often was she seen with a volume of Victor Hugo as her companion; it was said, too, that she paid great attention to the works of Voltaire and Lamartine. As an accomplished linguist, she was able to read most of the works of literary merit in the original. She spoke and wrote fluently and even elegantly German, Hungarian, Czechish, Polish, Roumanian, Italian, Romanic (modern Greek), English, and French, besides Latin and ancient Greek.

As she took up new studies from time to time, she engaged as her teachers men well known and renowned. One of these, Mr. Russo Poulos, Oriental Professor at the Vienna University, was her Greek teacher and reader, and he has written an interesting article about the linguistic attainments of the Empress.

„It was in a lovely spot,“ he writes, „where the palace of the Achilleon now stands, that Her Majesty first lived in a tiny house, near the village of Gasturi. Here, amid the olive groves, with a distant view of Corfu and the Albanian mountains before her eyes, she became enchanted with the Greek scenery and language. She visited every historic spot, and made endless excursions in the hills. For nine months she studied Greek, and when she knew the modern language she desired also to be acquainted with the ancient tongue.“ In 1889 Mr. Russo Poulos went to Corfu, where Her Majesty studied Greek throughout the whole winter. She learnt rapidly, and her sympathy with the Greek people aided her greatly. During voyages to Tunis and Malta her studies were pursued unremittingly.

The poems of Christopoulos Balaurides were especially beloved by the Empress; she read the Odyssey in modern Greek with ardour, and also studied some works of Heine in the same language. Although only engaged for one year, Mr. Russo Poulos remained for three, and Her Majesty attained the highest proficiency in modern Greek. The Emperor was often present at the lessons, and followed his wife's progress with interest.

She was perfectly at home when in the society of scientists, poets, painters, and artists in general; and although her early experience in Vienna did not contribute towards making the capital a favourite spot with her, still she loved it as the centre of literature, art, and music; and she bestowed her sincere friendship on many men of letters, painters, and musicians, and numbered Wagner, Liszt, Makart, Munkacsy, and many others amongst her intimates. The paintings of Munkacsy especially impressed her very strongly, and she frequently visited his studio and remained for hours in conversation with him. He is a fine-looking man, tall, broad, and erect, inclined, if anything, to stoutness; his dazzling white hair is brushed back, so that it stands all on end, and his white beard is combed out somewhat truculently. His cheek bones are high, his eyes small and deep-set, his skin and lips of unusual thickness. His name was originally „Lieb," but in 1874 he was created Count Munkacsy - Munkacs being his native town. The story goes that he began life as a carpenter; but this employment being uncongenial to him, he soon found his way into some studio at Pesth, then at Vienna, and lastly in Munich. He is now one of the most celebrated painters of the century, and commands very large sums for the sale of his pictures, of which perhaps the best known is „Ecce Homo," so greatly admired in England.

On similar friendly terms was the Empress with Makart, and many hours did she spend in his studio, which in itself was an art museum.

In science she took great interest, and frequently commanded lectures at her apartments. She studied politics, although she never took an active part in them, and also national economy. Her views were extremely broad, and Dr. Max Falk, who taught her Hungarian, and was a constitutionalist of the advanced school, tells us that she astounded him one day by asking him abruptly, „Is it also your opinion that the only sensible form of State government is the Republican?" „What suggested this question to Your Majesty," stammered Falk. „Oh," rejoined the Empress, „it is a question which I often used to discuss with Count Maylath, and I should like to know what you have to say about it."

She was perfectly open-minded in respect to social and political issues calling for solution. Although her inherited instincts caused her to be against democratic governments, she was still keenly perceptive by the light of present-day thought and intelligence of the failings and drawbacks of personal government.

She joyfully welcomed learned societies, and it gave her unalloyed pleasure to entertain them. In 1862 there met in Vienna the International Society of Jurists (Juristentag), and upon the initiative of Her Majesty all the members were hospitably received at Schönbrunn, and it was observed on that occasion how well informed the Empress was even then, at the age of twenty-five, and how she entered into animated conversation with various men of great renown, showing no mean amount of knowledge in that branch of science.

Such admiration did she win at that time, that spontaneously a demonstration was prepared to do her public honour, and on the 25th of August a monster torch-light procession moved to the suburban castle, the torch-bearers consisting principally of the members of all the learned societies of Vienna, of foreign guests, and of philanthropic and art institutions, etc., making a mass of more than ten thousand persons. The Mayor of Vienna was received by the Empress on the balcony of the imperial residence, where she accepted a large bouquet of flowers from his hands, which was offered as a token of the people's esteem and love, and as a mark of admiration from men of letters and of scientists and artists especially. Elizabeth, in replying to the short speech of the Mayor, said that the memory of that day would always be one of the most valuable, and that she felt most honoured by the ovation. She was indeed greatly touched by the demonstration, which so clearly showed that she was appreciated by men of learning and lovers of science.

Her love of knowledge was no doubt inherited from her father, and was again visibly transmitted to her children, whose turn of mind runs distinctly in the same groove. The late Crown Prince was an ardent student, especially of natural history, and both Princess Gisela and the Archduchess Valerie are interested in science and art to a great extent. Her Majesty's selection of persons who should superintend her children's education showed her good sense and liberal ideas. Bishop Ronay, the Hungarian, to whom was entrusted the education of the Archduchess Valerie, has given to the world in an interesting little work containing his reminiscences the instructions given to him by the Empress personally. „I wish my daughter to be initiated in all sciences of the day. I prefer that she should have only one teacher - yourself," said the Empress to the Bishop. „I want her to be educated on religious principles, but by no means in narrow-mindedness and fanaticism. Let her be taught to the widest extent by that great teacher of us all - Nature."

To her Greek studies the Empress was, as we have before intimated, very devoted; and having mastered the language, she loved to surround herself with men and women who shared with herself a love of classic lore - like Dr. Christomanos and many others.

In music she was proficient on the piano, and later in life took anew lessons from Abbé Liszt, for whom she had the greatest veneration. She considered it a special privilege to be allowed to play with him in duet. The *Rhapsodie Hongroisie* his composition, was one of her most favoured pieces. Wagner she admired, but perhaps more as a poet than as a musician. Rubenstein was also a great favourite; but Chopin touched her most strongly, and she never tired of playing or hearing his Nocturnes, which are so full of deep feeling.

A more simple instrument upon which she liked to play, and which was taught her by her father, was the Alpine zither. She played it remarkably well and with great expression, such as one would hardly believe could possibly be drawn from so simple a contrivance as the zither. She performed on various occasions at charity concerts, and was certainly far above the average amateur musician. It was one of her most distinct characteristics that whatever she undertook she carried to a successful issue, and her tenacity was well known. She was also the happy possessor of great patience, and her readers tell us that when the reading of a new novel or any literary production was commenced she never would allow it to be left unfinished, even if it bored her. „One never knows," she used to say, „what it may be - the ending may be good enough to make up for the poor beginning."

It was one of the highly esteemed prerogatives of the imperial lady to seek out struggling young artists and *littérateurs* and afford them such assistance as would allow their talents to have full scope; and many were her personal pensioners who gratefully and lovingly worked in Rome and other art centres, in the hope of rewarding their noble patroness at some future day by a life-long devotion and gratitude. But what she did was from feelings dictated by her conscience, which told her that it was her duty in her position to assist in the development of talents which a Higher Being than herself had planted in the hearts of recipients of her bounty: sufficient reward did she find in their success.

Her exalted position and her wealth, combined with her love and admiration for the fine arts, made her naturally a great patroness of artists; and her personal collection of pictures and statuary, as well as of other works of art, was perhaps one of the finest possessed by any private person.

Certainly it can be said that the Empress Elizabeth occupied a high place in the world of science, literature, music, and art, and that her tastes were distinguished by a chastity and elevation rarely to be found at the present time; but especially remarkable was the variety and Catholicism of the subjects which arrested the attention of this imperial scholar and the wide scope of her interests and studies.

CHAPTER VI.

THE EMPRESS AS AN ARCHITECT.

There is traceable in the race of the Wittelsbachs a very strong propensity to create architectural monuments, to beautify and build. Ludwig I. of Bavaria changed Old Munich into a modern Athens, his son Max continued the work, and the fantastic Ludwig II. left behind him palaces and castles not rivalled in grandeur and magnificence in the whole world. The same spirit constrained the Empress Elizabeth to erect palaces which should be her own conception and would exactly suit her tastes. It was for this reason that Her Majesty, although having at her disposal more than fifty residences, castles, and villas, craved for structures with which she might be fully identified and individually connected, which should be her own property, and represent as much as possible her ideal; and in this way arose such palaces as Lainz near Vienna and the Achilleon in Corfu.

At her coronation in Hungary the nation presented their Queen with the Castle of Gödöllö, and this has remained ever one of her favourite residences. However, I do not intend here to speak of this country seat, which was also her hunting-box: I mean to devote this chapter only to the two buildings which she herself conceived, planned, and completed, and which stamped her as an architect of the noblest taste, and proved her love for the beautiful, pure, and simple. That she was greatly influenced when building the Achilleon by her love for Greece, ancient and modern, is evident; whereas Lainz, which represents the modern architectural school, shows us that her appreciation of beauty was not narrowed or limited to one style. Very few even of those who know Vienna will have ever seen the beautiful retreat of the late Empress at Lainz. Although within driving distance of the capital, one might believe it to be many miles away in the country. The grounds are laid out by the cleverest of landscape gardeners, and seem many times more spacious than they really are. The flower gardens are magnificent, especially in the early spring, when they are filled with the finest varieties of hyacinths and tulips.

Large beds of lilies-of-the-valley and violets simulate a carpet and are a triumph in that style of gardening. In the summer there is a great variety of lilies to be seen, and the show of chrysanthemums in the autumn is also most lovely. The palace itself is comparatively small, but by clever contrivance it was made to accommodate the suite of the Empress, which, even when cut down on a visit to Lainz, was of goodly numbers.

A peculiarity of the house is the chapel, if I may call it by this name. The Empress had arranged in the hall an alcove, which contains an altar, upon which every morning Mass was said by one of Her Majesty's chaplains. A large mirror, which can be moved by a hidden spring, glides from wall to wall, and generally covers the alcove, so that no trace of an altar is visible.

The Empress's bedroom contains a beautiful replica in pale pink Sicilian marble of the Niobe in the Uffizi Gallery in Florence, surrounded with ferns and miniature palms, the whole being lit up by small electric jets during the night.

But the better-known architectural work of Her Majesty is the villa which she erected in Corfu, and which she called, after the Homeric hero Achilleus, the Achilleon. As far back as 1861, when she had

64

spent a winter in Madeira on the advice of her physicians and returned in the late spring to Trieste, she visited on her way the Island of Corfu, and remained there some days, staying at the Villa „Mon Repos," then the summer residence of the Lord High Commissioner for the British Government, which was placed at her disposal. She at once became greatly charmed with the semi-tropical scenery; and becoming more and more enchanted with it, felt a great desire to build an establishment for herself on this charming isle.

Corfu is best known to those who have studied Greek history and read the poems of the immortal Homer as Corcyra, and is supposed to be the Scheria where Ulysses in his wanderings found the Phasacians.

It was on these shores where Nausicaa, the most charming maiden that ever turned her fingers to homely housework, took her father's clothes to wash, and escorted the much-tried warrior within reach of security. It was on this island that Ulysses gave much of the remarkable and almost incredible history of his wanderings. In more recent times Corfu was known as Corcyra, the headquarters of the innumerable pirates who in those days endangered navigation. As early as 229 b.c. the island came under the sway of the Romans. We

ACHILLEON.

ACHILLEON.

find little recorded of the history of Corfu up to 1205, when it was in the possession of the Venetians till 1797, with the exception of one century. From 1807-1814 it was occupied by the French, and fron 1815-1863 it formed one of the seven islands of the Ionian League under a British Lord High Commissioner, till at last in November 1863 it was incorporated in the kingdom of Greece.

Elizabeth purchased the ruined Villa Braila, near Gasturi, situated on a wooded hill - a most charming spot, from which a very fine view is obtained of the blue stretch of ocean, the undulating verdure-clad slopes of the island, and the distant shore of Albania.

In the Bay of Gasturi the Empress built a jetty of white marble to facilitate the landing from her yacht. Near the landing-stage stands a white building, the engine-house for the generation of electricity used for the lighting of the park and castle, and hence in straight line between ever-blooming orange trees and mighty cypresses and olives a road leads up to the palace. The whole mountain is covered with thick vegetation, and beside the semi-tropical foliage can be seen the black oak and the yellow broom, while the ground is covered with anemones and daisies.

As an entrance to the park there are erected most artistic wrought-iron gates, and on passing through one finds oneself at the foot of marble terraces; there is a large ornamental fountain, and graceful staircases lead on both sides up to the terrace; marble steps lead up higher and higher, till an antique temple is reached, which the mistress of the Achilleon consecrated to her favourite poet, Heinrich

66

TEMPLE IN THE PARK OF THE ACHILLEON.

Heine. White columns support a cupola crowned by an angel holding a wreath of laurels in his hands. Under the cupola there is a life-like statue of the singer of love and woe; worn out he seems, sitting in an armchair, his knees covered with a woollen coverlet, his head sunk upon his breast, and with eyes which appear to be filled with tears he looks out upon the blue sea and upon the far-stretching purple mountains; in his hand he holds a scroll, upon which there is written:

HEINRICH HEINE.

> *What means this lonely tear?*
> *It still dims my view,*
> *So many years*
> *It lingers in my eyes.*
> *Thou lone and lingering tear,*
> *Dissolve now also.*

The work was done by a renowned Danish sculptor, Louis Hasselriis, in Rome, who, himself a warm admirer of the poet, has put much spirit into the statue. All round the temple there are ancient cypress and gigantic olive trees. Behind the temple is situated what may be called the most beautiful wild park which the sunny South and the art of the landscape gardener could create. Various roads and avenues lead hence up to the White Palace, which takes its name from that hero who was a type of everything that was noble, powerful, and grand in the classic history of Ancient Greece.

As soon as the Empress had decided to build a home for herself on that classic ground, she consulted the inspired word-pal liter of ancient lore, Alexander, Baron of Warsberg. It was he who first designed the plans for the palace, which the Empress afterwards altered according to her own idea.

The situation is unique: the Empress selected the site herself, and created upon the ruins of the old villa the Achilleon, with a magnificent peristyle, atrium, and a garden of muses. Raffaele Carito, a celebrated architect of Naples, changed the ideal plan of the castle into such an one as could be carried into modern reality. However, nothing was done without the full consent of the Empress, who was in daily consultation with the architect. The Achilleon lies to the south of the capital. Doric is the predominant type of architecture, with a slight intermixture of Ionic. The colonnade on the east is especially fine, and is ornamented with frescoes of great artistic beauty. The subjects chosen are Apollo and Daphne, blind Homer reaching for his lyre, Theseus and Ariadne, and Aesop, surrounded by an entranced multitude, reading his fables to them. The colouring of these pictures is most remarkable and rich.

It was only possible for an empress, and only for such an empress as Elizabeth was, to build a palace as we see here in its superb whiteness standing in its dark green surroundings. The grounds are ornamented with the finest statues procurable, both antique and modern, amongst which perhaps the most beautiful are those of the Dying Achilleus and the Peri (Byron). The rooms Her Majesty used are situated on the third floor, which opens on to the hill side, and leads into the Garden of the Muses - a square surrounded by high cypress trees and statues of more than life size. Her Majesty was thus enabled to step out into the grounds without disturbing any of her household. In these apartments she was entirely alone. In the storey below there was a suite of rooms for the Emperor and another for her daughter Valerie.

I will endeavour to describe the palace, as far as words can do so. In front there is a grand portico,which leads into the open atrium; heavy purple velvet curtains divide the outer from the inner colonade, the floors being inlaid with many-coloured marble slabs, whilst a most graceful and light staircase leads to the upper storeys. The hall is adorned with frescoes representing dancing nymphs, and is turned almost into a winter garden through the presence of many fan-shaped palms stretching up to the ceiling. Here is the smoking-room, a library, sitting-rooms, and the dining-room for the household; alt are of fine dimensions and in pure classic style, as far as the demands of the present render it possible. The staircase is in the Greek Pompeian style; a large skylight allows the light to fall down and show to full advantage the colossal fresco painting which fills one whole side of the walls, representing the Triumph of Achilleus as he is dragging the corpse of Hector round the fallen walls of Troy.

The apartments of Elizabeth herself are the most ideal one can imagine; and the spirit of poetry-melancholy ever makes itself felt. Everything here she has endowed with her own individuality; every piece of carving, every painting or statue, was selected by herself. The rooms are in accordance with the descriptions of those said to have been occupied by Penelope and Helena; even her bedstead, which stands only about eight inches from the floor, is shaped according to the descriptions contained in the ancient epic; the four posts are adorned with smiling wood nymphs, and a rich silken cover is negligently thrown over the white linen sheets and pillows.

The most valuable and chaste collection is formed by the statues which adorn the so-called Garden of the Muses; they are mostly works of the classic art which were brought from Rome, where the Empress purchased them from Prince Borghese. There is one statue here, not practically belonging to this classic company, which is Canova's „Third“ Dancer, for which it is rumoured the lovely Princess Paulina Borghese, sister to Napoleon I., stood as a model.

The Dying Achilleus is by the Berlin sculptor Ernest Herter. The Empress also erected a statue of Lord Byron in memory of that Anglo-Greek patriot and singer.

Even the furniture was made, according to the strictest instructions of Her Majesty, from the designs of Professor Caponetti in the Albergo dei Poveri in Naples. Here one finds lovely chairs inlaid with silver and ivory, covered with sheep's fleeces; also beautifully polished tables, sofas, and other ornaments, like those mentioned in Homer's poems, or made after the models which were excavated in Pompeii and Herculaneum.

One of the favourite spots in this fairy-like scene was the terrace, over which there was spread an awning of antique cloth. On a wind-exposed corner there was fixed Aeolian harp; and one view was of the blue sea; while a marble bench formed in a half-circle reminded one of the ancient Greek seats, as we see them so frequently represented in the pictures by Alma Tadema.

Here we are reminded of that wonderful artificial cave built by King Ludwig II., at an enormous cost, at the Linderhof; the Empress having had constructed a similar cave, the entrance to which is almost covered with maidenhair ferns of gigantic size. On the background of the interior large mirrors throw back a misty green light, and a small rivulet descends with its melancholy murmur. Nymphs and fauns seemed to have had a particular charm for the romantic and somewhat fantastic Empress, and the park and gardens are dotted with statues of that class.

Here, in this secluded paradise, the exalted lady spent many months of the year, accompanied by her youngest daughter, and visited at short intervals by the venerable Emperor. Willingly did she give up her days to those who loved her; but the nights were her own; and when all was still, and the moonlight was bathing the scenery with its hazy silver, the Empress could be seen wandering through the gardens, ascending the mountain tops, promenading the avenues, or standing in deep contemplation before one or other of her favourite statues. After the death of her only son, the Crown Prince Rudolf, in 1889, she erected to his memory a monument in one of the most enchanting spots of her domain, and here she was frequently found standing in deep thought and meditation, forgetful of the passing time, when the first rays of the rising sun threw their light upon the gardens.

She was idolised by the people of the island, her kind, sympathetic heart often constraining her to visit the poor fisher-folk's homes; and soon would her affability, her sweetness of temperament, and her charm of manner brighten up the poorest hut; but never did she leave those whom she found in need without giving sufficient to at least alleviate their sufferings for some time to come. „The Queen of the Achilleon" she was called first by the inhabitants of the neighbouring

71

villages, but later she received the appellation of „The Recluse of the Achilleon." When she went through the villages the people rose, and blessings were showered upon her, and women often would run to her to kiss the hem of her dress.

In her last will and testament the late Empress has left the Achilleon to her elder daughter, Princess Gisela of Bavaria, and Lainz to the younger, Princess Valerie.

CHAPTER VII.

THE EMPRESS AS A SPORTSWOMAN.

In our own country the Empress was best known before her death as a great sportswoman. From her very first youth riding was one of her greatest pleasures, and well was she known in the hills and dales surrounding her paternal castle. After she had become Empress she was able fully to indulge in this passion, and her stables in Vienna and Gödöllö contained the finest studs to be found in Europe. It was she who introduced fox-hunting into Austria and Hungary.

Her Majesty herself hunted for many years in Hungary, making Gödöllö her headquarters. Her figure became very famous at the celebrated meets of Kaposztas Magyar. It is well known that there are no people in Europe more accustomed to riding than the Hungarians, a child hardly ever reaching the age of four without being able to keep itself on a horse's back. The introduction of fox-hunting by Queen Elizabeth created quite a sensation, though now there are several packs regularly hunted by Hungarian noblemen. It is certain that within twenty years fox-hunting will be as popular in the land of the Magyars as it is in our own country. In fact, it has been even introduced in mountainous Tyrol, where the Sporting Club is now keeping and hunting a good pack.

However, the sport never was the same as it is with us, and nothing therefore was more natural than that the Empress should have desired to come to England to participate in the national sport here. She was a thorough-going huntswoman: in Meath, Cheshire, and Northamptonshire she enjoyed to the full the excitement and pleasures of hunting. She first came to England twenty-one years ago, and hunted with the Pytchley Hounds, of which Earl Spencer was then the master. She took Cottesbrook Park in Northamptonshire for six weeks, and I cannot do better than quote such an expert as the late Mr. H. O. Nethercote as to the impression the Empress left behind her.

„It was at once remarked by the large field, which respectfully saluted her on her first appearance with the Pytchleys, that her seat on horseback was extremely graceful, that her hands were perfect, and when the hounds began to run in earnest that there was no fence big enough to stop her."

During her stay at Cottesbrook Park the Empress was present at all the best-known fixtures, riding three horses a day, which enabled her to hold her own against the best-mounted and the best-nerved. It was entirely through her instrumentality that the Hoffinghill Steeplechases, near Brixworth, were revived, and to the funds of that hunt-meeting she was a munificent subscriber.

Whilst sojourning in the county of Meath, which was in the second year of her hunting-season in our islands (1879), she was accompanied by Prince Liechtenstein and piloted by the late Captain „Bay" Middleton. She usually rode a fine chestnut mare, and wore a dark blue riding-habit with gold buttons, a high hat, and white scarf. There was a strange peculiarity observable - namely, that she used to carry, besides the crop, a small fan in one of her hands, which she used after a run was over. Among the gentlemen in the field were Captain „Jock" Trotter, Earl Spencer, Lord Randolph Churchill, Lord Killeen, General Eraser, the Honourable H. Plunkett, the Honourable H. Boscawen, and the Honourable Henry Bourke. The Empress rode exceedingly well, frequently taking and keeping the lead, and carrying away many a brush. She had only one serious accident during her hunting in Ireland, and this was when riding The Widow, when she had a really big fall, but fortunately was not seriously injured.

The country in which the Meath Hounds met is the largest in the United Kingdom, stretching from Cabra Castle in Louth on the north, to Woodlands, the seat of Lord Annaly near Dublin, on the south, and from Lough Sheelin in West Meath to the seacoast on the east. This enormous tract is nearly all grass, and among the finest land in Ireland.

When Her Majesty came first to Northamptonshire in 1878, she brought her own stud from Hungary; but soon she became greatly interested in and enamoured of Irish hunters. The lamented death,

74

shortly before her arrival, of Charles Brindley, the popular huntsman of the Ward Union Stag-Hounds, had enabled the Empress's agent to purchase the celebrated grey mare which had carried Brindley so magnificently in many a difficult run.

In no Irish county has fox-hunting existed so long or been brought so nearly to perfection as in the county of Meath, for which thanks are due especially to Mr. Samuel Reynell of Archerstown, who it was that studded Royal Meath with gorse coverts. He was succeeded as master by Mr. Waller of Archerstown; but after five years he gave way to the finest rider that Meath ever saw, Captain „Jock" Trotter, who, although a Scotchman by birth, had become to all intents and purposes an Irishman, and was one of the most popular men there.

The Empress seemed never able to express enough praise for the hunting in Ireland, and returned there the following year, and, had it not been for the political disturbances which at that time made Ireland the hotbed of outrages and agrarian crimes, she would no doubt have returned there every year; as it was, she came again in 1880.

She always travelled under the title of Countess of Hohenembs, and was attended by a large suite. She had procured as her hunting-box a house at Summerhill, by no means a palatial home, but splendidly situated for the purpose for which she had hired it, where, it was reported, the first thing she did upon her arrival was to visit the stables and give a carrot to each of the hunters forming her stud there. So great was her passion for the field, that, in spite of the long and fatiguing journey from Vienna, she was out the very day following her arrival, and hunted with the Ward Stag-Hounds.

Lord Langford was at that time master of the Wards, and amongst those who participated in the sport were such well-known men as Leonard Morrogh, Colonel Forbes, and the Earl of Mayo. Captain Middleton was again the Empress's pilot; and although he was perhaps the most difficult man to follow. Her Majesty used to do it without ever failing. She was one of the most straight and hard-riding women with hounds; and in the first week she, Captain „Bay" Middleton, and Bayzand, the personal attendant of the Empress, were all unseated in accidents in the field. Amongst her favourite hunters were Domino, Cameo, Hard Times, Doctor, and St. Patrick, and it was often noticed that a peculiar affection existed between the hunters and their imperial mistress.

An Irish lady who frequently accompanied the Empress in the field writes: „She was a most thoughtful and judicious rider, and eminently considerate for her mounts. I have seen her jump off with the lightness of a fawn when a check or a wait at covert side permitted, and almost unassisted shift her saddle slightly, always taking care that it was well clear of the play of the shoulders, and then from the pocket out would come sundry dainties, with which her favourites would be smilingly indulged.

„Her hands were the smallest I ever saw, and her hair the longest - it fell around her like a cloak when unloosed; and I think I may add my own testimony that the heart which the dread assassin pierced was one of the kindest that ever beat in human breast.

„Arrived at the meet, we were told that the Empress had already come, and had gone to put on her habit at the neighbouring house; so there was time to leave the carriage and go about greeting friends. I remember that Lord Combermere was there, and Sir Philip Egerton, and the veteran sportsman Mr. Nathaniel Cooke.

„It was frequently after eleven o'clock when the Empress came upon the scene, riding a good-looking bay mare; and with her was Lady Rocksavage, whose mount was a dappled grey. Her Majesty on this occasion wore a silk hat, rather low in the crown, and a dark blue habit, with a collar of sable fur; her gloves were of strong tan leather.

„She always was riding a level-seat saddle, cut away at the withers and neatly flapped over; and in the pouch at the side were sundry bits of biscuit and lump sugar, with which she occasionally fed her horses."

The last run the Empress enjoyed in Ireland was on the back of St. Patrick, and she often deplored her inability to hunt again in that paradise of foxhunting. She came to Ireland without any pretensions of State, and her master of horse was Prince Liechtenstein, a smart, wiry, good-looking Austrian, not young, but well preserved, his small pointed beard just showing a tinge of grey, and his keen, deep-set eyes a few wrinkles at the corners. He was a brisk and fearless horseman, was a pleasant conversationalist, and spoke English perfectly. The Empress seemed very nervous about her *début* in Irish fields, and tried her best to avoid the crowd of gazers which always collected in the grounds of her hunting-box.

Another lady who also frequently had the pleasure of hunting with Her Majesty says:

„The Empress had an exquisite figure, and her riding-dress was the admiration of every field which she graced whilst visiting in Ireland. So closely did her well-cut skirt cling to her form that it was a common saying among ladies that she must be ‚sewn into it,' and that they did not believe she could dismount; while her jackets, of absolutely perfect build, were fitted to a twenty-inch waist of exquisite and natural rounding. She either wore a high silk hat or a small Tyrolese hat of pliable felt, dented slightly in the centre of the crown and furnished with one little up-standing wing. I never saw her wear a flower or a neck-bow, or a pocket-handkerchief protruding from the front of her bodice. Her dress was simplicity itself, and its only noticeable adjunct was a black-and-yellow fan, very light and portable, and about as plain as it was possible for it to be. This was carried either in her hand or in a little slip strap in front of her saddle, and it always came out at covert side, and very frequently when trotting along the roadway. ‚Afraid of her complexion,' the Irish ladies said; but it was not so at all; no one ever guessed the wherefore of it, and this is my own very first mention of the matter. She had an absolute dread of the itinerant photographer and of the sketcher, ever on the watch to snatch impressions of her truly lovely face.“

She paid a short private visit to Ireland two or three years ago, her time being almost entirely spent in the West. She was always mindful of the poor people; in the district where she stayed, and her acts of benevolence are fondly remembered in many a lowly cottage in Meath and Kildare.

As an instance of the indomitable pluck of the late Elizabeth of Austria I may give the following incident, which occurred during her stay in Meath.

After a long run the hard-pressed fox jumped over the wall of Maynooth College, and rushed across the exercise ground where the students were pacing to and fro, evidently absorbed in pious contemplation (Maynooth College is an institution for the preparation and study of the Roman Catholic priesthood). The sight of a fox in the grounds roused the sporting instincts of the young clericals, inherent in most Irishmen, and they were on the point of giving chase when the wall was again cleared, this time by a beautiful woman on a spirited horse: it was the Empress of Austria, who had followed the fox through thick and thin, and evidently through water as well, as the dripping state of her habit testified.

Dr. Walsh, now Roman Catholic Archbishop of Dublin, and then the head master of Maynooth, received the imperial hunts woman with due courtesy, and, observing the danger which she ran of getting chilled in her wet clothes, suggested a wrap. Her Majesty willingly accepted the offer. But now arose a difficulty: there were no feminine habiliments to be found in that training establishment for young priests, and she had to make use of Dr. Walsh's academic gown, which she laughingly threw over her shoulders, and, after having partaken of refreshments with the president and professors, rode home. The Empress seemed so pleased with that accidental visit and the hospitality shown to her by the reverend gentleman, that shortly after she came again on a longer visit to Maynooth, and there, as elsewhere, charmed all by her grace and affability.

On that occasion she presented Dr. Walsh with a beautiful diamond ring, and after she had returned to her home in Austria she sent the college a fine statuette in solid silver of St. George and the Dragon, and also a suit of vestments richly wrought of silk and gold, and covered all over with shamrocks worked in green silk.

She certainly made many women friends in Ireland; and it is a strange coincidence that in a letter to an Irish lady, written only a few months ago, she alluded to her sister's awful death at the bazaar fire in Paris, and remarked that she felt a presentiment that some tragedy was in store for herself.

Her Majesty's last hunting season in this country was in 1881, when she rented Combermere Abbey in Cheshire for two months, from the

18th of February. She entrusted at that time an Irish horse-dealer with the task of buying hunters for her; and when she arrived at Combermere Abbey she found a superb stock of Irish horses awaiting her, with her principal huntinggroom, an Irishman of the name of Tom Healy, in charge.

Combermere Abbey, Lord Combermere's seat in Cheshire, has long been tenanted by famous sportsmen, and is a good specimen of a nobleman's country seat in the North of England. No better choice could have been made, since from there it is feasible to easily reach both the Cheshire packs, Sir Watkin Wynn's, the North Staffordshire, and the Shropshire. As usual the Empress's hunting-stud comprised about thirty horses. Her pilot here was Colonel Charles Rivers Bulkeley, who, in addition to being a brilliant horseman, knew the whole country well, and proved himself an admirable guide. One of the finest runs in which she participated was from the Bache House covert to the hills, in which even the magnificent horse upon which she was mounted proved none too fast. With reference to her horses, hardly one of which ever put a foot wrong, they were trained until it was almost a wonder that they were not sick of jumping and declined to face a fence at all. There was a special etiquette observed when the Empress was one of the field - namely, that no one should ride in front of her or her pilot; and even if, owing to a turn made by the hounds, Her Majesty and her leader were not at that moment in front, those who were, were expected to fall out of the way; while it was also customary for Lord Spencer, Captain Parke Yates, Mr. Corbet, or any man with whom the Empress might be hunting, to approach the imperial visitor hat in hand, and ask whether it was Her Majesty's pleasure that the hounds should draw again.

Amongst her horses were Florae, Timon, and Ashtown. She generally consulted, when buying horses, Mr. Edward Macdonald of Ashtowngate, and Mr. Allen McDonogh, then of Athgarvan Lodge, Curragh, who ranked at the time among the best judges of horse-flesh and the Very best horsemen of the day. They are both dead now, as is also Captain Middleton, who was killed while riding in a steeplechase.

The Empress's liberality was generally remarked upon; she made presents with great freedom, even the station-masters on the smallest wayside stations through which she passed were remembered and surprised by the receipt of a pin, ring, or some other present of value.

EMPRESS ELIZABETH OF AUSTRIA.

At the close of a season, and as a token of the great pleasure afforded her, the Empress gave a prize, to be competed for by Northamptonshire farmers; and when the prize had been won, Her Majesty gave a luncheon party, at which the Prince and Princess of Wales, the late Duchess of Teck, Earl and Countess Spencer, and many others were present. Her graciousness and affability were most marked; and her grooms and stablemen, for the most part Irish, absolutely worshipped her. She proved to be a practical horse-woman, and likewise a humane one.

At the end of her first season in Northamptonshire, the Archduke Rudolf, Crown Prince of the Austrian Empire, came on a visit to England, Scotland, and Ireland, enjoying the field sports of the country. He was, in company with the Prince of Wales and Prince Louis Napoleon, a guest of the late Duke of Hamilton at Hamilton Palace in Lanarkshire. The purpose of his visit was to bring his mother home to Austria.

The Empress was obliged, on account of failing health, to give up riding in 1882, and she felt the deprivation very much. She took up fencing, in which graceful art she became very proficient; she also tried her hand at fishing, but that sport proved too slow for her active and restless temperament. She was an intrepid mountain climber, and a strong and skilful swimmer. One of her great pleasures was mountaineering; and up to the very end of her life she was accustomed to take long walks, frequently tiring her cavaliers and ladies without feeling fatigued herself. Her Majesty's hunting establishment in her own country was at the Castle of Gödöllö, near Buda-Pesth in Hungary. There she kept a fine stud and a pack She loved the ocean; the stormier it was, the higher the winds and waves, the better pleased Elizabeth appeared to be. She generally remained with the captain on the bridge during the severest gales, and no remonstrances against her exposing herself to danger were of avail. She only shook her head, and bade her attendant go down into the cabin; but she herself kept to the bridge as long as the gale lasted.

MIRAMARE.

The Miramare is a paddle steamer of an old design; but her lines are greatly admired by experts and yachting people, and all her appliances are of the most modern style, the saloons and cabins being furnished according to Her Majesty's own suggestions. The yacht is very swift and graceful, and has accommodation for a large retinue; on the deck arrangements were made to enable the Empress to indulge in her pleasure of walking exercise.

CHAPTER VIII.

THE EMPRESS AS A TRAVELLER.

„We change the surroundings,
but a heart bleeds under
all social variations."
George Moore.

Although the area over which the Empress Elizabeth travelled appears limited in comparison with the known extent of the world, and in consideration of the facilities now offered to wander through it, she at least thoroughly saw and knew the different lands which she visited.

Soon after her marriage she accompanied her husband on an extended tour through the various provinces of the Austrian Empire and through Hungary. In September 1856 she visited the magnificent mountain fastnesses of the Alpine countries, Styria and the Tyrol; and on this occasion she climbed the highest mountain to be found in the Alps, the Grossglockner. The excursion was made from Heiligenblut, where their Majesties had been staying at the rectory. At four o'clock in the morning they were present at Mass, and knelt devoutly before the altar, the Emperor in the national Tyrolese costume, his spouse in a short woollen skirt, shirt, and light jacket.

Accompanied by a few experienced guides, they commenced the ascent, the Empress and the majority of the suite on horseback, the Emperor always on foot, in order to lose no point of vantage. When they were about six thousand feet high, the Emperor plucked a most beautiful Edelweiss near a rocky precipice, and handed it to his wife with these words: „This is the first time in my life that I have plucked the Edelweiss myself." The Empress enjoyed the magnificent and far-extended view with almost child-like pleasure. How small appeared to her the mountains around Possenhofen which she knew so well, and how grand was this enormous pile of rock on the top of which she now stood, looking down upon the low-lying towns, villages, lakes, and mountain scenery! A hut which is built near the top of the peak for the convenience of mountaineers has been named in memory of the ascent by the Empress, „Elizabeth's Rest"; and the highest peak of all, which the Emperor alone ascended, has since then been given the name of „Francis Joseph's Height." The party returned to Heiligenblut at one o'clock. Up to the time of her death the Empress took pleasure in referring to this excursion of her youth.

After this the Empress travelled to Marburg and Graz; hence they undertook a journey to Venice and Milan, where their reception was so hearty and spontaneous that the Emperor exclaimed, „This wipes out the memories of 1848!" and, turning to his wife, said, „Your charms have done more to win these people than all the bayonets and cannon of my armies." Again they undertook a journey through Hungary, which lasted fully four months. Unfortunately the health of the Empress suffered at that time, and it was decided in 1860 that she should go to Madeira and spend a winter there. Queen Victoria offered to lend her one of the royal yachts, the Empress not possessing one at that time, and Elizabeth made her first journey to Madeira on board the Victoria and Albert. The warm climate of the South soon restored her health, and she returned on the 24th of May, 1861, quite well and strong; but in June of the same year she had a relapse, and therefore left Vienna on the 20th of that month, and sojourned at Miramare, near Trieste, whence she went to Corfu, where she stayed for some time. She returned via Venice, went to Reichenau, and from there to Kissingen, where she remained until the end of August 1862.

I have already mentioned that she made Corfu her home for some months during every year, and from that place she made various excursions in her yacht, the Miramare. In 1880 she undertook a more extended journey to the Orient, and remained for some time at Zante. Jt is told that, when on a pedestrian expedition to a villa which was not far from that town, she met an old peasant woman, who was the caretaker of the mansion, and was living in a small, poorly furnished hut near by. The Empress entered the humble abode, to the great surprise of the old woman, who told Her Majesty that she was sorry she could not show her over the villa, as the owners were absent and had taken away the keys, but she begged that the lady would accept a glass of fresh water from the sparkling spring of the neighbourhood. The Empress accepted with thanks. When she had entered the hut, she noticed a poor crippled boy - the only living being the peasant woman had to bestow her love and care upon - endeavouring to leave the only room in the cottage for the open air; his position touched Her Majesty's sympathy, and she immediately gave the woman a princely present of money, in order that she might be able to take better care of the child. When the poor mother saw the gold pieces, she must have guessed who her visitor was, for she fell upon her knees and kissed the hem of her dress, overcome by gratitude and joy. The companions of Her Majesty, who had been witnesses of this deed of kindness, were deeply touched by the pathetic scene enacted before them.

During this journey she also visited Troja; and it may be remarked here that the Empress was the first European sovereign who did not mind the difficulties and fatigue which had to be endured in order to visit this historically celebrated spot. On that occasion some of the Turkish guards who accompanied the caravan were about to shoot some of the wild geese which were found there in large quantities, thinking that the sport would give Her Majesty pleasure; but she forbade them; she did not approve of such cruelty, and opposed the wanton killing of harmless animals merely for the sake of personal gratification.

In 1887 the Empress visited England. She stayed for some time in the Isle of Wight, having taken Steephill Castle, and afterwards in Norfolk. Her repeated visits to England and Ireland in 1879-82 I have touched upon in another chapter.

Very frequent were her tours through Bavaria and various parts of the Salzkammergut, and her favourite spots for sojourning at were Feldafing in Bavaria, Wiesbaden, Kissingen, and Ischl, where she held Court for many years during the summer months, and whence she ascended the renowned mountain of that neighbourhood, called

„Schafberg." All these places, however, she visited more rarely every year, and even at the imperial castles she only remained a short time. During the last few years of her life she visited Biarritz and the Riviera very frequently, always travelling under the name of the Countess of Hohenembs, an incognito which was generally respected by the people with whom she came into contact. When at Cap Martin she rose at a time when nobody stirred at the hotel, when the birds in the trees and bushes round the hostelry commenced to sing their morning songs, when the sun had hardly begun to kiss the blue ocean out of its nightly slumber. She used to leave the hotel accompanied only by a lady-in-waiting, to make a long tour on foot in the neighbouring mountains, from which she hardly ever returned before noon to her breakfast.

HOTEL AT CAP MARTIN.

One morning, only two years ago, while staying at this place, she surprised the visitors at Monte Carlo by appearing amongst them in pedestrian attire, attended by a lady-in-waiting and a chamberlain: upon her return to her hotel at Cap Martin for breakfast, she had walked a distance of sixteen miles!

She was always dressed in simple black, with a large dark straw hat upon her head, a sunshade and a fan in her hands. Her romantic and poetic nature enabled her to see in every small flower a rich treasure of beauty. The Empress Elizabeth was essentially a lover of nature, and found both joy and grief in the contemplation of her charming surroundings. She loved to rest at great heights, dreaming, meditating, and trying to forget the woe which was gnawing at her

85

heart. Here she loved especially to read her favourite poets, and here she felt in close communion with them.

For some time she was accompanied on her mountain expeditions by the little Archduchess Valerie, and her sister, the Countess of Trani.

In 1883 she resided for sometime in Baden-Baden, and in the same year she came to Styria for the autumn. Here it was that she almost lost her life by an accident during one of her excursions. She was riding over a wooden bridge which spanned a deep ravine, called „The Dead Woman"; she had got half-way across, when the horse stumbled, both forelegs slipping through a hole in the bridge. The situation was a most dangerous one, but eventually the Empress succeeded in jumping off her horse, pulling it out, and regaining her saddle once more.

It certainly seemed that, ever after her great grief in 1889, the Empress was possessed almost of a mania to rush from place to place, getting tired of one as soon as she had settled there, and ever seeking fresh scenes: at one time it was her palace in Corfu, then some watering-place in Germany, a large hotel on the Riviera, a lonely chateau, and again a crowded hostelry, in Switzerland. She was a familiar figure in nearly every one of those Baths in the centre of Europe in which women especially seek relief and deliverance from the miseries of diseased bodies and diseased minds. Kreuznach, a beautiful little town in a valley only half an hour's railway journey from Bingen-on-the-Rhine, is a favourite place for women, and is supposed to alleviate their manifold troubles. This resort was visited by the Empress, and her habits there were as peculiar as elsewhere. She would get up about four o'clock in the morning, and by six had completed that two hours' walk before breakfast which is part of the cure. Early as the people of Kreuznach were, there was nobody about at that hour in the morning. The next walk was between nine and eleven - again a time when few were about, as most of the patients were then either at their breakfasts or in their baths.

The Empress did not care to be seen by anybody; she shrank from the vulgar and embarrassing stare to which royalty is generally subjected.

At Territet in Switzerland, which was also a favourite resort, she followed similar habits; there she used to take her bath punctually at five o'clock every morning; then she sat on the terrace until eight o'clock, when she was served with a breakfast of iced milk and biscuits; and during the rest of the day she would roam about, dressed in black, with short sleeves, a short skirt, and tan boots. She hardly ever wore gloves, and when passing any one she invariably covered her face with a fan. On returning to her apartments, which were extremely simple, she would respond to the respectful salutes of her suite with a gentle wave of her hand. She always retired to rest very early. At Kissingen in Bavaria, where she stayed as late as April of this year (1898.) - a time before the season had begun, and when therefore few people were about - she walked a good deal, usually alone, and sometimes she would even enter the shops and buy a great many articles that attracted her fancy; generally, however, she allowed this to be done by her ladies-in-waiting. Some people who saw her then state that there were still traces of the dazzling beauty of countenance which she once possessed, and that she preserved much of the unquestionable grace of her figure.

Of late years she travelled with only two ladies-in-waiting and one chamberlain in attendance, and her suite was therefore very limited.

During this year (1898) she had accidentally seen some photographs of the Dolomite region in the Tyrol, and was informed that an hotel had been built in those mountain fastnesses near the Karer See, right under the hill of the „Rosen Garten," not far from the Rothwand. This renowned district receives its name from the enormous quantity of rhododendrons which grow there, and also from the lovely pink colour of the mountains, which seem to glow into a fiery red at the rising and setting of the sun. It was soon after Her Majesty had become acquainted with this region that she made her appearance at the Karer See Hotel, and occupied rooms there for some weeks, making extensive excursions in all directions; and there are few peaks in the neighbourhood which the Empress did not ascend.

She seemed on all her journeys to be at war with the police authorities, as it was most uncongenial to her to be watched and guarded by detectives, and she would frequently go so far as to give false information as to her intended journeys.

Paris the Empress visited frequently, but never in an official manner. She was expected to go there in state during the time of the Empire, shortly after the famous interview between Napoleon III. and the Emperor Francis Joseph and herself and Eugenie in 1869; for some reason or other she did not do so. But the imperial lady often came to Paris in a quiet, unostentatious manner, and usually took many rides in the Bois de Boulogne, and did extensive shopping in the Rue de la Paix or on the Boulevards.

Early in 1898, before starting for her villa at Cap Martin, she stayed in Paris in the Hotel Dominici with the Countess of Trani. This was for the purpose of being able to visit the sinister spot in the Rue Jean-Goujon, where her youngest sister, the Duchesse d'Alençon, perished in the flames at the Charity Bazaar. Later on she intended to go to M. Morot's studio, in order to see the portrait of the Duchesse, but a violent attack of neuralgia obliged her to hasten her departure for the South.

The Empress of Austria was well known at Amsterdam and The Hague, where she was considered somewhat eccentric. She was accustomed to walk about the capital alone and unattended. Once, as she was promenading with a large yellow fan before her face, a jocular passer-by snatched away her fan and cried, „Come, let us look at your face." Much diplomatic commotion resulted from this incident.

Favourite journeys of Her Majesty were those to Greece and Northern Africa and the Adriatic Littoral, where she was generally accompanied by her youngest daughter.

During her sojourn at Algiers she paid a visit to the old capital of Tlemczen and made many excursions to Staueli, the great Trappist establishment, and watched with the greatest interest the making of scent from rose geraniums, with which the monks are principally occupied. Here again she left a large money present for the benefit of the institution, having ascertained that many of the poor of the neighbourhood are fed and taken care of there. But it was not only in foreign lands that she enjoyed these long excursions; both at Vienna and at Buda-Pesth she used daily to drive out for some miles, and then leave her carriage and walk along lonesome wood-paths; and the people who met her had no idea that this slim figure in black, walking so unostentatiously, accompanied only by one lady, was their Empress.

The neighbourhood of Buda-Pesth has hardly a spot where the Hungarian Queen has not been. In October 1897 she spent a few weeks there attended by Fräulein von Kerenczij, her reader, and visited the celebrated grave of Gul Babas, the Mohammedan saint. Architect Wagner, the owner of the adjacent villa, accompanied the Empress, and explained to her the various remarkable points of the tomb. Indeed, there was nothing which would not awaken the interest of this traveller.

It was a strange feature in her character that she loved to be alone, and would even prefer to dispense with her lady-in-waiting and chamberlain. Only two years ago, when sojourning in Biarritz, she gave no little trouble to the Spanish Government by her frequent long excursions on foot across the French frontier without any male companions, as special precautions had to be taken for her safety, brigands not having yet entirely disappeared from that district.

The difficulties of those who were told off for her protection were by no means insignificant. For instance, the Empress Elizabeth, when in Paris, would often rise before five o'clock in the morning, and start for the Bois de Boulogne or elsewhere on foot or on horseback, and the detectives, who had been on duty around her temporary domicile all night, were compelled to follow as fast as they could. One of the police commissaries who looked after the Empress at Vichy states that, whilst she was kindness and amiability personified, she was incredibly imprudent, and often rather querulous about the measures taken for her security, in spite of the utmost tact and discretion on the part of those directed to watch over her.

One day the Empress, while climbing the hills round Mentone, was suddenly frightened by the hangdog appearance of a long-haired shepherd, and she was then rather glad to find herself protected. However, she very soon forgot this incident, and again asked for the suspension of all supervision. The detective, in reply to this request, explained that he was obliged to do his duty, and that he was moreover on the look-out for a suspicious character from the Danubian principalities, who was expected to arrive in the neighbourhood at the same time as the Emperor Francis Joseph; so at last she acquiesced in the arrangements.

In the Tyrol she took up her abode principally in Meran, where she was joined by other members of the imperial family, and where also her brother the Duke Charles Theodore with his family owns a villa, which they occupy during the winter months. There the guide Buchensteiner won the special confidence of the Empress, not so much on account of his thorough acquaintance with the mountains, as because he understood her so well, and knew how to keep back the Curious crowds who were anxious to see her.

In 1889, in spite of the unfavourable weather, she made some long excursions, and showed herself on these occasions a splendid pedestrian. Even in climbing the steepest hills upon bad roads she did not show any fatigue; in fact, it was sometimes difficult for her suite to follow her; and it was on that account perhaps that she undertook a great many expeditions lasting the whole day accompanied only by Buchensteiner, who used to carry a satchel containing some dainties and some milk, which would comprise Her Majesty's luncheon. This guide knew all the best spots from which fine views could be obtained, and there the imperial lady used to take a seat upon a stone or a stump of a tree, and look out on the beautiful scenery for hours and hours without one word being spoken.

I had occasion a short time ago to have a conversation with Buchensteiner, who said most characteristically: „When I take persons up in these mountains, I often marvel what they want up here; they do not seem to care for the view, they do not love the flowers or take any interest in anything - all they want is to be able to say they have been on the top of that peak. How different it is with the Empress; she overlooks nothing, - every stone, the most insignificant plant or flower, she observes; the most common bird, even a butterfly, seems to afford her pleasure; and when she comes to a spot whence she can look upon the beautiful expanse of scenery below, I have seen tears in her eyes, and a saintly look come over her as she gazed toward the blue sky, as if she were thanking her Creator for having accorded her this happiness."

When the Empress was at Meran last autumn (1897), and had taken rooms at the Hotel Kaiserhof, Buchensteiner was immediately commanded to wait upon her.

Here is an episode which may find a place in this chapter. The Empress Elizabeth had expressed a wish to arrive at Meran entirely incognito. However, her arrival, in spite of precautions, had become known on the same day. To the many enquirers at the hotel as to what time she would arrive it was answered, „At seven o'clock in the evening." An enormous mass of people crowded the approaches to the railway station and the Hotel Kaiserhof at that time, when a lady, in simple black dress, with a stick in her hand, walked unobserved along the street, and entered the hotel from a side door; it was the Empress, who had arrived many hours before, and had just returned from a mountain excursion of which not a soul knew anything. However, the wish of Her Majesty to be left alone was fully respected by the natives, and it was only the foreigners who, without any consideration, almost mobbed her when she went out in the daytime.

On the 2nd of November, 1897, the Empress visited the tomb of the Habsburgs at the Church of the Capuchins in Vienna, and prayed for some time beside the coffin of her never-to-be-forgotten son, the late Crown Prince Rudolf; and shortly afterwards she left the capital for Biarritz, where she remained until the 18th of December, 1897; and then went for a sojourn of some days to Paris, where she underwent a course of massage on account of slight rheumatism in one of her feet. She spent Christmas in the French capital, and was seen on various occasions walking along the gay Boulevards with her sister. On the 29th of December she arrived at Marseilles, where her yacht the Miramare awaited her, and in company with the Countess Trani she sailed for San Remo. There she remained with her sister up to the ist of March, 1898, and then went to Turin, where she again remained for a couple of days, and thence to Territet. On the 18th of April Her Majesty went to Kissingen, where the Emperor visited her on the 25th of the same month, coming from Dresden, where he had been the guest of King Albert of Saxony for the celebration of that personage's seventieth birthday. The Empress remained at Kissingen until the 8th of May, and journeyed thence to Brückenau, to drink the waters. Her sojourn there lasted a month.

On the 13th of June she returned to Vienna, and was there received by her husband at the railway station, with whom she drove to her private castle of Lainz, where she remained until the 2nd of July, on which day she journeyed with the Emperor to Ischl, accompanied by her daughter Marie Valerie and her husband and children. It was also on that day that it was officially made known that the health of the Empress was such as to give cause for serious uneasiness, and that it would be necessary for her to spend the following winter in a southern climate. The official notice stated that the Empress was suffering from anaemia, nervousness, and insomnia, and that the diagnosis had shown a slight enlargement of the heart. Her physicians had advised her to go to Bad Nauheim; and on the 16th of July, accompanied by her lady-in-waiting the Countess Sztaray and her personal medical attendant Dr. Kerzl, she arrived at that watering-place in Hesse, and took apartments at the Villa Kracht, placing herself under Dr. Theodore Schott, of whom I have already spoken. Her recovery was most remarkable, due partly no doubt to the fact that the visitors fully respected the Empress's desire for quietness and solitude.

On the 2nd of August she received the Empress Frederick, who came from Kronberg, and the interview lasted for more than half an hour, during which the most animated conversation was sustained. On the 23rd of August she met the Emperor William II. and his wife; and besides these the young Grand Duke of Hesse, and his charming spouse, the granddaughter of our Queen; paid their respects to Elizabeth.

So much better did Her Majesty feel, that there remained little doubt that her full recovery was assured, and that it would only be a question of time. She was advised to spend some time in mountain air in order to recoup her strength, and it was on this account that she went to Switzerland and returned to Territet, where she had already spent March and April. She arrived at that beautiful mountain resort on the 29th of August, and stayed at the Hotel Caux, near Glion. Here she intended to remain for some weeks before returning to join her husband in Vienna, during the festivities which were in preparation for the Jubilee of his reign. She had just returned from a visit to the Baroness Rothschild at her charming villa, and was on her way back from Geneva to Caux, when she was assassinated.

Dr. Christomanos, formerly reader to the late Empress, speaking of her many journeys, tells us of the following remarks she made to him some time ago: „I prefer travelling in the night, as then the illusion is greater - otherwise one must struggle with the hours before one reaches one's goal." When he once observed to his imperial mistress that it is said monarchs do not know the value of money, the Empress Elizabeth replied that she valued money as only, in her eyes, it should be valued - viz. according to the intensity of the wishes it gratified. „All things," she said, „should be paid for according to their worth to us individually. There is nothing of absolute value around us. I would give more for a book that I wanted and for a flower high up in a hedge than for a house or a journey in Algeria."

Whilst in a Kabyle village the Empress saw a white figure suddenly appear out of the darkness. It followed her, dodging about behind trunks of trees. „I recommended Her Majesty to return," says Dr. Christomanos. „She refused," saying, „No! the Arab would think we feared him. We might give him in this way bad thoughts. One should never stand in the way of one's destiny. The same instant the Kabyle stood before us, his manner being very threatening. The Empress did not for one moment lose her presence of mind. She said, „That is a madman. We must hasten away; such people are more dangerous than criminals."

On travelling through Venice the Empress remarked sadly, „The Emperor still speaks good Italian; that is all that is left of our kingdom - more than we need. I was also obliged to learn Italian, but I could not reconcile myself to this tongue, and all the trouble would have been thrown away."

Her Majesty travelled generally with a very limited suite, and had an allowance of about £ 5,000 per month for the purpose. After what has been said it is not difficult to judge how much of this sum went into the pockets of the needy.

CHAPTER IX.

THE EMPRESS ELIZABETH AND KING LUDWIG II. OF BAVARIA.

Considering the very extraordinary behaviour of the late Bavarian King Ludwig II. towards the lady to whom he was betrothed, and who was the youngest sister of the Empress Elizabeth, it strikes one as strange to find that an almost romantic friendship existed between him and the consort of Francis Joseph, which lasted to the very days which preceded the King's deposition and his tragic suicide.

The engagement of Princess Sophie of Bavaria with the King was popular, the more so because it was well known that the couple loved each other, and that the affair was not the outcome of diplomatic or political negotiations - the marriage would be a love match pure and simple. The sudden breaking off of the engagement without an explanation or even an apology ended the friendship existing between the parents of his intended bride and the King; but however strained the relations between them, it did not prevent the Empress Elizabeth from maintaining the most intimate friendship with the King, which was quite characteristic of her, as she never allowed herself to be guided by circumstances, and always acted upon her feelings, regardless of what others thought. That a relationship between such a poetry-loving sovereign as the King of Bavaria and an idealist like the Empress should have been most romantic seems but natural.

There is almost in the middle of the Lake of Starenberg, on the shores of which Possenhofen and the Castle of Berg are situated, an island, which, from the magnificent rose gardens which a former king had planted thereon, has received the name of „Rosen-Insel" (Isle of Roses). The island is reputed to have possessed in the most ancient times a heathen temple, which was later on converted into a Catholic chapel, and even at the present time Roman coins, vessels, and ornaments are found there. The gardens, which were first laid out by King Max, were greatly beautified by his son Ludwig II., whose love for all that was beautiful is so well known. It is said that there were sixteen thousand plants of this queen of flowers, and the scent was so strong that it could be perceived miles out on the lake. In the midst of these labyrinths of roses there stood a villa, called „Die Ermitage," the only dwelling on the islet, with the exception of a small cottage for the gardener's use. High hedges, formed of trees and bushes, surrounded the whole island so thoroughly that it was impossible to get even a glimpse of the gardens when passing in the boats; it was almost impossible to perceive the small jetty, built for the landing of the King from his steam yacht Tristan. In this small villa, built in the Italian style, which comprised only a very few rooms, Ludwig II. spent some of his most happy and quiet days; here he collected his favourite poets, and here he dreamt and meditated, and here he had his special rendezvous with the Empress Elizabeth of Austria, who, when on her yearly visit to her parents' Castle of Possenhofen, would meet the youthful monarch, and together they would indulge themselves undisturbed in conversation congenial to their tastes. From the upper storey of the building one of the finest of views can be obtained over the deep blue lake and the purple mountains which stretch as far as the eye can reach. To describe the gardens themselves would be almost an impossibility: the endeavours of two kings resulted in a collection of the finest specimens of roses known to the world; and their rich colours - white, yellow, and all shades of red, from the lightest pink to the darkest crimson - formed a lovely relief after the pure blue of the waters.

In the last year of his life King Ludwig visited the island rarely, and only when he knew that the Empress was staying at Possenhofen. It was so arranged that the two exalted personages should come to the islet at a given hour; but if anything happened to prevent their meeting, the one who had arrived would write a letter and place the same in a special drawer of a writing-table of which only their two Majesties had keys, and so they were able without the intervention of a third person to communicate with each other when a personal interview was impracticable.

After the death of Ludwig II. the villa upon the Isle of Roses was visited by the commissioner who had charge of the affairs of the departed monarch, and in the writing-table in question there was still found a letter, which had the following address: „The Dove to the Eagle." It transpired that these were the appellations used in their romantic intercourse, the Empress being the Dove and the King the Eagle.

Even at a time when Ludwig would not suffer a single soul to be near him, when his passion for solitude had almost become a mental disease, he was ever ready to receive his cousin and was happy to spend some time with her in conversation. There existed without doubt a great affinity between them, and it was often remarked that no one but the Empress appeared to understand the fantastic King, and the similarity of their ideas, tastes, and pleasures was strongly and frequently in evidence. How much the imperial lady sympathised with the unfortunate King, how deeply she felt his deposition and his tragic end, can only be conjectured; but the fact that she retired

EMPRESS ELIZABETH OF AUSTRIA.

immediately upon hearing of the catastrophe to one of her castles, in order to be able to give herself up completely to the grief which the tragedy had caused her, says much. For many weeks she mourned in solitude at the Achilleon.

The intimate and friendly relationship between the two was openly recognised at the lying in state of King Ludwig at the royal residence in Munich. Surrounded by the pomp displayed on such occasions by the Roman Church, combined with that prescribed by royal courts, the body lay upon a catafalque of sombre velvet, wrapped in a gorgeous purple mantle belonging to the order of St. Hubertus. Tall silver candelabra, holding burning wax tapers, stood in double rows at the side of the bier; next to this there were beds of flowers, formed by the many tokens of love and grief sent from all parts of the world; but there was only one floral tribute nestling upon the breast of the departed King - a simple spray of jessamine, the last gift the Empress of Austria made to her friend and kingsman Ludwig. More than once after his death did the royal lady visit the spot where the King lost his life, and she herself took great interest in the memorial chapel which is to be erected there. When visiting Possenhofen, she never neglected to make a pilgrimage to the Castle of Berg, or to pray at the spot where the unhappy high-minded Ludwig ended the life which had become intolerable to him.

The Emperor, the Crown Prince Rudolf, and his sister the Princess Leopold of Bavaria were all admitted to the friendship of the eccentric King, and Francis Joseph was fully aware of the great sympathy which existed between his wife and Ludwig.

It is reported that the Empress most strongly opposed the deposition of her late friend, and had actually prevailed upon the Emperor to promise to frustrate it, or at least to make it only temporary; the premature death of the unfortunate monarch, however, put an end to the matter.

CHAPTER X.

MATER DOLOROSA.

„But the whole life of man is full of grief,
Nor is there rest from toils."
Euripides.

A highly sensitive nature feels most acutely the ordinary troubles and worries of life; and how terrible must be the suffering of the sentimentalists with strongly sympathetic hearts, when they are allotted more than the common share of its bitterness!

The Empress Elizabeth of Austria was one of those, one may well say, unfortunate beings for whom the Germans have so perfect an expression, which we lack in our own language - *viz.* Gefühlsmensch („sentimentalist" - although this term by no means expresses exactly what is meant by the German appellation). She suffered intensely not merely the ordinary vexations which form part of every one's life, but she felt also the pain of others as though it had been her own.

When we consider the unusually large number of misfortunes and awful catastrophes which were crowded into her life, we shall experience no difficulty in understanding the vehement grief and sorrow which the sorely afflicted woman suffered for so many years. Nor can we feel surprised that on the blotter generally used by the Empress were written Byron's true words:

Count o'er the joys thine hours have seen,
Count o'er the days from anguish free,
And know, whatever thou hast been,
This something better not to be!

Early in her married life (1857) she had to mourn the death of her first-born, Princess Sophie. The imperial couple had undertaken a tour through Hungary. The Empress, in fulness of love for her children, could not separate herself from her two little daughters, and

99

it was therefore decided that they should travel with their parents. To guard against bad water on the journey, bottles, filled with wholesome spring water from Schönbrunn, were carried in the imperial train, and placed in ice, in order to be kept fresh and cool. However, from some unexplained reason, the water decomposed, and the child Princess, attacked by typhus, succumbed to this terrible scourge after a few days' illness.

In 1859 the Empress again passed through a time of great anxiety, her gallant husband being with his army in Italy, fighting in defence of his realm against the allied armies of France and Italy. The disasters of Montebello, Magenta, and Solferino produced unspeakable anguish in the sensitive heart of Elizabeth. A few years afterwards she wept over the body of a beloved cousin - the young daughter of the Archduke Albert, commander-in-chief of the Austrian armies, and hero of many battles - who, when on the point of becoming the wife of the Crown Prince of Italy, had met a terrible death by burning in her father's palace in Vienna, through setting fire to her light summer attire.

That the morganatic marriage of her eldest brother with Fräulein Mendle, an actress of Munich, also caused the Empress great grief is certain, for she was warmly attached to him; and as she could not entirely disapprove of a match founded on such a romantic love, she especially felt his being obliged to resign all his rights and privileges on account of his matrimonial arrangement.

The number of morganatic marriages contracted by her near relatives was extraordinary, and the Empress felt the many shocks her proud husband experienced by the actions of the imperial archdukes no less strongly than the mesalliances of her own family. The Archduke Henry married Mdlle. Leopoldine Hofmann, who sang in the theatre of Graz, Styria. But long before him the Archduke John, brother of the Emperor Francis II. and great-uncle of Francis Joseph, had set an example of this new departure in the imperial house by marrying a peasant. The story is quite romantic. One day he arrived at the post-station of Brandhofen; the postmaster was greatly embarrassed, for he found all his postilions (the name given to the drivers of the diligences) absent, and was unable to supply one for His Imperial

Highness, who was anxious to continue his journey at once. The postmaster's daughter, Fräulein Anna Plochel, conceived at once the idea of disguising herself as a postilion and driving the Prince; on the way he detected this disguise, became fascinated with her youthful beauty and the pluck she displayed, and ere many months had passed married her. She was created a Baroness of Brandhofen, and later Countess of Meran; and her only son is now the Count of Meran, and still lives in Styria.

But the saddest episode in the chapter of mesalliances is that known as the mystery of Johann Orth, one of the most remarkable romances in the dynastic history of Europe in this century. The Archduke John Salvator of Tuscany, and a nephew of the Emperor Francis Joseph, had fallen in love with an opera-singer, whom he married in spite of all family opposition,renouncing at the same time all his rights, privileges, and rank, and assuming the name of Orth, after one of his castles. The romantic marriage was celebrated secretly, but in a perfectly legal manner, by the Registrar of Islington, and countersigned by the Austrian Consul-General in London. Johann Orth next bought in Liverpool a fine ship, which he rechristened the *Santa Margarita* after his wife; and so anxious was he to guard against the vessel being recognised, that he stipulated that all drawings and photographs of it should be handed over to him, and these he burned with his own hands; moreover, he caused all portraits and negatives of himself and of his wife to be bought up at any price, and these were likewise destroyed. I am giving here only absolute facts.

Shortly afterwards he set sail with his wife for South America, and the vessel was duly reported to have arrived at Monte Video and departed for a destination unknown. But from that moment every trace was lost of the ship and all on board; not a scrap of any sort of news as to her fate has ever been recovered, although many a search has been made along the coast by order of the Emperor of Austria and his Government. Adventurers, treasure-seekers too, have been at work, as it was well known that the Archduke had on board over a quarter of a million pounds in gold; it is believed that he intended to have bought an estate in Chile with the money and to have settled there, but that the vessel foundered off Cape Horn during a terrific storm which raged on the coast shortly after the ship left. From time to time since then the most startling rumours have been published about the missing Archduke having turned up: one being that he had been one of the leaders of the Chilian rebellion, having divided his treasure among his crew, burned his ship, landed on a lonely coast, and made his way to Chile; another that he was the famous marshal who fought in China; a third story tells that the eccentric Prince is still alive, and secretly corresponded with his mother until her death quite recently; but no doubt the truth is that the *Santa Margarita* lies at the bottom of the sea, and that all on board perished.

Again was the life of Her Majesty saddened by the disastrous events in Bohemia in 1866, followed in 1867 by the appalling catastrophe at Queretaro, where a brother of Francis Joseph, who had accepted the crown of Mexico, was executed as a traitor. The horror of the event was heightened by the fact that the wife of the ill-fated sovereign, who had returned to Austria in order to seek succour for the hard-pressed Emperor, lost her reason on hearing of her husband's death, and that at the very moment he was being led forth to execution on the other side of the world his brother Francis Joseph was being proclaimed under circumstances of unprecedented splendour King of the Magyars on this.

The unfortunate lady has lived for twenty-nine years at the Castle of Laëken, near Brussels, where she finds her only solace in music. She is a sister of the King of the Belgians, and was born in 1840, and married when only seventeen years of age. Elizabeth was a most kind friend to her sister-in-law, and visited her frequently whenever she was in a fit state to receive her: no journey was ever too long for her late Majesty when she felt that she could alleviate the sufferings of others.

Before I reach the climax of the Empress's sufferings, which brought about such a terrible change in her whole life, and from the shock of which she never fully recovered, I may again refer to the death of Ludwig II. of Bavaria in 1887, which was a source of such genuine grief to her. Strongly, too, did she feel for her sister the Countess of Trani, who was left a widow by the suicide of her husband in a fit of temporary insanity. The sad experiences of another of her sisters, the ex-Queen of Naples, she followed with her sympathetic heart, and mourned with her the loss of her throne; and only a few years ago her tears were again shed in sorrow at the terrible disaster which befell her youngest sister, the Duchesse d'Alençon, who in trying to save the lives of her young companions sacrificed her own in the appalling fire at the Charity Bazaar in Paris.

The extent of the Empress's sympathies will be understood when it is mentioned that she suffered intense grief over the death of the Duke of Albany, whom she had on various occasions met in Vienna and England; and that she felt the sad decease of the Duke of Clarence on the eve of his intended marriage with the Princess Mary of Teck so strongly that she was obliged to withdraw for a few days entirely from intercourse with even her nearest relatives. Always of a romantic nature, it was natural that this melancholy event should have made a particularly strong impression upon her, the more so as it followed so quickly the death of her own son, at which the young Duke had displayed so much grief.

Those who have suffered can best understand the feelings of grief in others, and it was for this reason that the Empress was so intensely sympathetic with the Prince and Princess of Wales, for whom she entertained a great regard; in fact, close bonds of friendship existed between them. I retain a vivid picture in my mind of the Empress walking side by side with the Princess of Wales down the carpeted platform of Edge Hill Station when the royal party alighted from a special train. Elizabeth had been paying a visit to Liverpool, and incidentally to the delightful seat of Lord Sefton. They were a pair of regal beauties, and so remarkably alike in carriage, stature, and pose of head as to make the mistake of thinking them sisters quite pardonable; the only difference was that the Empress had a slightly firmer step than the Princess, and displayed more strength in the chest and shoulders. The Empress at that time was lithe and graceful in every movement, and alighted from the railway carriage with the activity of a girl of eighteen, rather than with the cautious step of a woman of forty-six, as she then was.

It caused the Empress great distress to hear of the death of the young Prince Imperial, the son of Napoleon and Eugenie; and her mother's heart went out in its fulness towards the lonely woman who once wore a crown and is now an exile in foreign lands. Shocked and grieved, too, was she over the murders of Lincoln, Garfield, and Carnot; in fact, no tragedy could pass without exciting in her sympathetic sorrow and grief. And lastly I must mention the great disappointment caused her by the elopement of her grand-daughter with a young Protestant officer.

One might feel induced to ask if anything could be added to such a list of misfortunes beating upon a woman who ever strove to do her duty and to alleviate the sufferings of others, and it is sad to say that this question has to be answered with a most emphatic „Yes."

The thirtieth day of the month of January 1889 brought upon the poor mother a disaster which may will be said to stand unique in this century. It is a strange coincidence that this day also is the anniversary of the execution of King Charles I., one of Prince Rudolf's ancestors. The Crown Prince Rudolf, who was the only son of Francis Joseph and Elizabeth, was at the date mentioned thirty years of age. He was spending some days at the Castle of Mayerling, his shootingbox, not far from Vienna, with a small suite and a few friends. On the evening of the day above referred to he was seen for some time in his box at the operahouse; thence he drove to his country seat, and on the last day of the month Europe was shocked by the news that the youthful Prince had died a violent death.

Many were the rumours accounting for this terrible tragedy; it is doubtful whether the whole truth will ever be known; and whether his death was caused by his own hand, or by the hand of another, is still an open question. What is known is that the Crown Prince was found dead with a terrible wound in his head in the early hours of the 30th of January, lying upon his bed; it appeared that the skull had been broken either by a stroke with some blunt instrument or by a pistol ball. In the castle there was also discovered the body of a young lady, the Baroness Vetsera, killed by a revolver shot. It was suggested that the unhappy Rudolf had committed suicide, but indications (the state of the wound itself) led strongly to a different surmise. However, of the two most generally accepted theories, one made the tragedy a case of double suicide, the other attributed it to the vengeance of a relation of the young Baroness, who, unable to challenge the Prince, killed him and shot also his paramour.

What this tragedy must have been to his mother it is impossible to tell. In the splendid isolation of thrones family ties are exceptionally close and tender, because sovereigns can hardly have friends. We know that here in England the death of Lady Augusta Stanley, the wife of the late Dean of Westminster, not a relation, but only a friend of our Queen, affected her almost as much as the loss of her husband, because Lady Augusta had been long about her person. The loss to a sovereign of a near relation, one of the few persons who can speak freely, must be great. But what must it have been to the Empress of Austria, already burdened by more than her full measure of misfortunes, in poor health, and of an exceptionally nervous temperament, to lose her son - her only son - whom she loved with all the intense love of which a mother is capable?

Her heroism on that occasion was extraordinary. She undertook herself the sad duty of informing the Emperor of the terrible news. Although her own heart was bleeding, the sense of duty was victorious in the wife; and the noble woman understood how to comfort her imperial spouse, and to alleviate his grief and suffering. With what intense admiration did the peoples of Austria and Hungary - nay, the whole world - look up to the exalted woman who sat upon the throne of the Austrian Empire, when, herself bowed down with unspeakable grief, she endeavoured to console and to support her husband, whose afflictions were so many and so terrible! But from that day the Empress Elizabeth was no more what she had been; her heart had experienced at that moment such pain that it became as dead; she could, when it was needed, be heroic towards the Emperor, but the more terrible was the reaction which followed, and which overwhelmed the sensitive heart. A dark shadow rested upon the beautiful countenance of the Empress; she was never known to laugh from that moment, and even her smiles became rare; a veritable Mater Dolorosa she wandered through the wide world, finding her

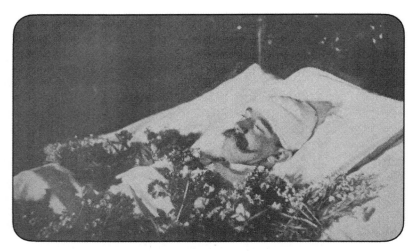

CROWN PRINCE RUDOLF LYING IN STATE.

only consolation in doing good to others, and in making their sufferings her own.

All sorrows of the past faded into insignificance beside her suffering and agony at the sad death of the Crown Prince. It was ever said that Elizabeth and Rudolf were more like brother and sister to each other than parent and child; and we can fully conceive how great were the pangs which rent her devoted and loving heart when she looked upon the pale face of the youthful Prince, who was the hope of her life and the centre of her wishes and expectations. The devotion of her youngest daughter, Marie Valerie, helped to assuage her grief; but the passage of nearly ten years had not been able to bring her forgetfulness. Never did she pass through Vienna without descending the crypt of the Church of the Capuchins, to lay a wreath on the coffin of her Rudolf - to kneel, her head resting on the silver lid, for hours in silent prayer; and she never left the city without paying a visit to the late Prince's shooting-box, and remaining there in prolonged devotion in the chapel, into which the room where the terrible tragedy took place had been converted, the castle itself having been turned into a monastery.

106

The grief of the Empress was expressed in her every action during the last nine years of her life, and It no doubt added much to the breaking up of her health; in fact, the wound which was inflicted upon her heart on that terrible winter night in 1889 was only healed by the assassin's steel on the loth of September of this year (1898).

CHAPTER XI.

THE RECLUSE.

„To suffer, and to gain thereby
A more exalted grade
Among the spirits purified by pain."
Robert, Lord Lytton.

That the Empress Elizabeth from her earliest youth loved the silence of nature, that she found happiness in wandering in the quiet and lonesome avenues of the park that surrounded her father's lake-side castle, or in the vast green aisles of a mountain forest, or in sitting on a mossy bank, reading one of her favourite authors, is well known; and when she was called upon to fill the position of mistress of the Court of Francis Joseph, although she took part in all the functions with grace and dignity, it was no secret that she would have greatly preferred to have been able to roam about alone or with her spouse, in some secluded spot where she could with him give herself up entirely and unrestrainedly to her love for the treasures offered by nature. She contrived to retire more and more from Court life, for doing which her state of health gave her excuse. After the festivities in connection with her silver wedding in 1879 she every year - appeared more rarely before the public, and when the death of the Crown Prince happened, her love for solitude became so intense that soon she could only find repose „far from the madding crowd."

Vienna saw her no more; her short stays there were given up to visits to the coffin of her son. Her private residence, the Castle of Lainz, which she had liked so much in former days, could not hold her for more than a week at a time: even this secluded spot was not quiet enough for her. In this strange passion we cannot fail to again trace a similarity with her kinsman Ludwig II, It may be said that her presence for the purpose of viewing the pageant which was arranged for the celebration of her silver wedding was actually her last public appearance. Already at the wedding of the Crown Prince Rudolf with Princess Stephanie of Belgium, which took place with great pomp on the 10th of May, 1881, at Vienna, it had been noticed how very reluctantly Her Majesty showed herself to the people, and only participated in such festivities as took place in the more intimate family circle. It is true she retained her interest in all those charitable institutions in the establishment of which she had assisted so successfully; she still continued to visit regularly hospitals and kindred establishments, and have personal intercourse with the sufferers; but she preferred Ischl to Vienna, and there she sought the society of

CROWN PRINCE RUDOLF AND CROWN PRINCESS STEPHANIE.

peasants in preference to that of the highest classes. Ischl afforded more perfectly the quietness which she needed. Her youngest daughter had been her constant companion up to the time of her marriage in 1890, when she wedded the Archduke Francis Salvator, the wedding being by the desire of Her Majesty quietly celebrated at Ischl.

Another drop of joy fell into the cup of bitterness when in 1893 her grand-daughter, Princess Augusta of Bavaria, the younger daughter of the Archduchess Gisela, married the Archduke Joseph Augustine. But no event was important enough to rouse her again from her lethargic state; she began to shun people; and when travelling every contrivance had to be resorted to in order to guard her from the stares of the many who found pleasure in looking upon her. So secret were her movements kept, that she had been residing for weeks at Miramare before her presence became known in Trieste, a large town situated only a few miles distant.

When sailing in her yacht, she could be observed promenading the deck alone for hours and hours; not a soul was allowed to approach and disturb her.

But more than anywhere else was she able to indulge in her passion for solitude when residing at her palace in Corfu. As I have already shown when describing the Achilleon in a previous chapter, her apartments there were completely isolated from any other part of the building; she had her private entrance, and could leave or enter the palace entirely unobserved at any moment during the day or night. Her meals she took by herself, waited upon only by a lady-in-waiting and one footman. She would spend a few hours during the day in the society of some of her suite, or with her teachers and readers; but the nights were her own - then she would wander alone through the dark groves and along the gloomy walks. When every one had retired and night covered the landscape, in the subdued glimmer of the moon or the stars, the Empress was often seen entering the gardens, clad in dark, closely fitting garments, a black veil thrown over her head, as she glided along the terraces and the paths of the park, and found her way to the beautiful monument she had erected to her son Rudolf in one of the most enchanting spots of her domain.

So far as it was practicable she had in reality become a recluse, and her desire to still more thoroughly bury herself in some place far from all she knew and had once loved was expressed to her intimates over and over again.

When her husband visited her from time to time during her sojourns abroad, she became more animated, and seemed to be imbued with new life; she appeared for the time being to forget her woes. But the reaction which followed such visits was very marked. When, shortly before her assassination, she was staying at Nauheim, she received, it is true, the visits of some exalted personages, as already mentioned in a previous chapter; but the interviews were of extremely short duration, and most of her time the afflicted Empress spent alone.

In a similar way she could not be prevailed upon to accept an invitation to the Court of Queen Victoria, when, a few years ago, she was for the last time in England, but only paid Her Majesty a flying visit. This is the more remarkable when it is considered that she entertained a great love and admiration for our beloved Queen, and for the Princess of Wales and Princess Henry of Battenberg. It had almost become a disease, this intense dislike to mankind, and it caused Francis Joseph great anxiety. The tragedy of Geneva becomes the sadder when we find that her health had improved so much during her stay in Switzerland that she had commenced to enjoy again the society of others, as was shown by her visit to the Baroness Rothschild, and by her decision to return to Vienna to participate in the Jubilee festivities with the Emperor.

This change was strange, as her aversion to step out of her solitude had some months previously reached such a pitch that even her meetings with her nearest relations became painful to her. Some years ago she was strongly attached to her brother Charles Theodore and his family, and she rarely missed her annual visit to his country seat, or failed to meet him at Meran, where he was in the habit of spending the winter with his family. Her niece the Duchess of Urach (who was the most studious of royal ladies, and so fond of books that it was difficult to persuade her to tear herself away from them to join in the social distractions of her position) was especially loved by her aunt, and yet even her society had become distasteful to the Empress. In fact, she preferred to live in contemplation and in the memory of happier days alone, in solitude - a recluse.

CHAPTER XII.

REMINISCENCES AND ANECDOTES.

„The fierce light that beats upon the throne" enables us common mortals to observe the doings of those occupying the highest positions, and, our interest in them being ever great, it so happens that we hear of innumerable tales and anecdotes, which, if not in every instance authentic, allow us nevertheless to judge the general characteristics of those of whom they are told; and on this account they deserve consideration.

I am not in a position to vouch for the truth of every item here recorded, but I have sifted the material at hand as carefully as I could, and may at least say, „Si non è vero ben trovato."[1] Neither do I pretend to observe a chronological order in repeating them: they are given as I received them. But so much I may state, - that some of them come directly from people who have been in the *entourage* of the late Empress; all from persons whose veracity I cannot doubt; and, finally, the truth of some has been generally accepted, although I by no means place myself unreservedly upon the side of the believers.

I refer more particularly to the stories which belong more or less to the occult and supernatural, but which I cannot forego repeating, for this work would appear incomplete without them, so essential have they become to the Geneva tragedy.

I may begin with a tale the action of which is laid in the first years of Her Majesty's married life. Accompanied by the Emperor, she visited an exhibition of modern paintings, mostly by young artists, and was requested by her husband to make some purchases, in order to encourage rising talent. It was the Emperor's desire that she should buy works on various subjects, but he left the choice entirely to her. In viewing the large collection she was accompanied by a lady-in-

---

[1] „If it is not true, it is well invented."

waiting, whose duty it was to mark those pictures in the catalogue which Her Majesty selected. When she had passed through various rooms, it was found that she had put the mark to about twenty or twentyfour pictures. When some weeks after those which were picked out arrived at the imperial palace, it was found that they consisted of twenty-four specimens, but instead of the expected variety of subjects they all treated of one and the same - namely, „horse-flesh." Elizabeth had been so completely carried away by her love for horses, that every work, without exception, represented her favourite animal in one way or another. A pleasant smile was observed on the countenance of the Emperor as he inspected the selection of his youthful consort.

A very unusual experience was afforded the Empress on a visit to the renowned lunatic asylum near Vienna. Having read of some hypnotic experiments made by a physician who was well known on account of various successful trials, and who had succeeded, in the case of a confirmed drunkard belonging to one of the best Austrian families, in inducing him by hypnotic suggestion to take the greatest dislike, even disgust, to alcoholic drinks, and to become by his own choice a teetotaller, Her Majesty became convinced in her own mind that this extraordinary power exercised by some individuals over others would lead to a most beneficial issue. She therefore presented herself at the asylum at a time when she understood experiments would be made. She followed every movement with the closest attention, and was satisfied with all she saw, although no actual practical results were derived from the trial, if we except the case of an old patient, who, when under mesmeric influence, spoke of the life of his youth, and thus enabled the authorities to identify him, which they had failed to do for more than twelve years, during which time the unfortunate man had been an inmate of the institution. The Empress repeated her visits on different occasions.

Police Commissary (Inspector) Dietze, who, during some years, was employed by the French Government to superintend the arrangements made for the safety of the Empress during her sojourn in Cap Martin, tells the following characteristic story:

One day Her Majesty commanded his presence at the hotel, and requested him to discontinue the police regulations in connection with her person. M. Dietze informed the Empress that under such circumstances he should have to ask for his recall, but she begged him to remain at Mentone, and added, „But I implore you to give your attention to the safety of my husband: his life is necessary for the weal of his subjects; but I am only an insignificant, griefstricken mother - nobody would care for my life. I may become the victim of an accident, but you cannot prevent a landslip when I am out on the mountains, and such accidents are the sole danger with which I am threatened; but for Heaven's sake watch over the Emperor - he has a noble and good heart - his life is valuable to millions of people."

Mrs. O'Donoghue, who knew and observed the Empress when in Ireland for the hunting season, tells some stories of those days, which are proofs of her affability, and of the interest she took in every one who came into contact with her. She says:

„I had the misfortune to ‚stake‘ my horse badly one day, and had to walk for a mile or so to Courtown, Captain Davis's residence in those days, close to Kilcock Station. The Empress Elizabeth was at lunch in the hospitable dining-room of the mansion when my entry was made; and here again the considerate Kaiserin evinced her womanliness and sympathy, just as the least pretentious of her subjects might have done. I can recollect the scene so well, - the lovely Empress ‚veritably‘ dismounted, and not looking in the least ‚sewn in,‘ and the ladies who were also present casting covert glances at her outer jacket, or little coat of smooth blue Melton cloth, which was laid across the back of her chair. When the time came to put it on, the Empress, helped by her courteous host, felt for some time in vain for the second armhole, and, moving her pretty hand about in search of it, said laughingly, ‚How awkward I am - how very awkward; you must excuse me!‘

„I think it worth mentioning, as indicative of the Empress's regard for animals, that on one of her Cheshire days she noticed a man riding with a terrible bridle, a strong wiry ‚rope-bit‘ attached to an ordinary snaffle; and it must have been excessively severe, for the horse's mouth was bleeding at both corners. The beautiful Kaiserin's sensitive eyes positively dilated when she saw it, and she uttered one word, in admirable English too - namely, ‚Brute!'

„I must either be silent respecting some lovely traits in the Empress Elizabeth's character and disposition, or occasionally place my own poor personality alongside of hers, which was majestic. In short, she was a kind friend to me in those happy early days; and when later on a lamentable accident stopped my hunting career for ever, her words of sympathy were the most tender that comforted me in my pain. I can never tell, not even to this day, why she deigned to notice me, for in truth I was ‚small and of no reputation,' and was moreover the very antithesis of her beautiful and stately self.

„She was riding one day over a rather rough bit of roadway, a short cut to some covert that was to be drawn, and as the going was slow a good many among the front-rank riders took the opportunity to speak a deferential word of welcome to the beautiful woman, who certainly adopted no pretentious airs. Purely from admiration of her I longed to do the same, and my heart was thumping against my breast with the effort to summon up courage for the ordeal, when the whole cavalcade got on to a better stage of roadway, and the chance was lost. But mark what followed. The Empress, escorted by Earl Spencer - who, I am sure, must remember it - slackened rein a bit, and, glancing round, addressed a pleasant word just when I was feeling particularly small, and then for one delicious moment I rode by her side and answered her prettily put queries respecting my experiences of Irish sport. She cared nothing to know them - how could she? But she evidently did care that a young rider with a flushed face and eyes of eager longing had been debarred from speaking to her when evidently yearning to do so."

A story which is still well remembered in the surrounding country of Possenhofen refers to an incident in the girl's life. On the expeditions in which she often joined her father, they would sometimes take rest and refreshment in a mountaineer's cottage, and on various occasions provided the dance music at Kirmesses (fairs) by playing zithers, which were easily procured for them, such instruments being found in every household in the Bavarian Alps. Once when the ducal pair had succeeded in preserving their incognito, they were offered and accepted some small silver coins in recompense for their services, and these the Empress treasured highly. „It is the only money I ever earned," she told a friend a few years before her death, when showing her some of her treasures.

As I have had occasion to remark before, the Empress displayed great taste in her dress; but for years she only wore black or white. Not very long ago she distributed among her intimate friends all her Court costumes and light-coloured attire; she said pathetically on that occasion that she would never feel gay enough to wear bright-hued dresses again. She had caused her wedding dress to be cut up and made into a suit of priestly garments for a church in Buda-Pesth: it was a white brocade woven with silver threads. Her bridal wreath encircles now an embroidered picture of the Virgin Mary in the Loretto Chapel, where the Empress frequently used to attend services.

Once the Empress saved the life of a poor woman in Hungary; it happened one day in November 1882, when Her Majesty drove to the meeting of the hounds near Magyarod; the road lay along some steep precipices by the side of the Raicos River; suddenly the Empress ordered the carriage to stop, for she noticed an old woman close in front of her walking straight towards the side of the road where the precipice was - a declivity of some hundreds of feet. Elizabeth, fearing danger, jumped out of the carriage, and was in a minute at the side of the old woman, took her arm, and led her away from the chasm. The poor woman was blind, and had been left alone for a moment, the boy who attended her having gone to fetch some water to quench his thirst. There is no; doubt the poor creature would have lost her life; and when her little grandson returned the Empress reproached him in strong terms for his thoughtlessness, gave the woman a few gold pieces, and continued her drive, having been detained for a quarter of an hour by the occurrence.

In 1887 the Empress spent some time at Cromer in Norfolk. One day shortly after noon she was walking along the coast, when she suddenly observed a large crowd of people congregated around some object, and on enquiry was informed that a railway porter of the Great Eastern Railway Company, named Walter Moules, had been accidentally drowned. The Empress enquired after the home of the poor man, and directed her steps there without delay, finding the wife and children at dinner. They had no idea of the misfortune which had befallen them, and in order to prevent any one telling the terrible news too abruptly to the widow Her Majesty called her to her side, and in the most considerate manner imparted to her the sad intelligence. She was just in time, for at that moment the dead body was brought to the house. With a promise to be a friend, the Empress closed her conversation with these words, „Pray for your husband and take the best care of your little ones,"and then left quickly. A few hours afterwards a lady-in-waiting appeared at the humble cottage of the grief-stricken widow, handing her in the name of the Empress a purse containing £ 400.

Around Gasturi in Corfu the tales of her benevolence are innumerable; but she especially endeared herself by her kindness to an anchorite, who had selected a small rocky islet in the bay as his abode. Well aware that it was his desire not to be disturbed by people in his meditations, the Empress used frequently to row all by herself in a small boat out to the island, in order to leave baskets with eatables for the hermit, and when absent her steward at the Achilleon was instructed to see that the man did not buffer for want of food.

A poor octogenarian, who had been for many years stricken with rheumatism, and had been at last reluctantly compelled to leave the hut in which she had spent all her life to enter the almshouses, was once spoken to by the Empress when visiting the institution. The poor woman expressed her grief that she was obliged to leave her old home, where she had hoped to spend her last days. Deeply touched. Her Majesty promised to see that she should return to her old abode, and accordingly the next day the old woman was removed to her former habitation, which had been made comfortable under the Empress's personal supervision, and here she lived for many years under the special protection and on the bounty of the mistress of the Achilleon. A gravestone, erected by her protectress, now marks the place where the poor creature is buried.

So many similar and well-authenticated instances of the murdered lady's beneficence could we give that a volume might be filled with them, but those related will suffice to show the beautiful character of the woman who, herself such a great sufferer, never tired of alleviating the lot of others.

A very pretty story is told of the late Empress's father, which, as it is in close connection with her birth, may find a place here. At Christmastide 1837 Duke Maximilian took a stroll through the grounds near his castle, when he met a poor old woman carrying a heavy bundle of firewood. He asked her why she carried such a large quantity, and she replied, „Well, sir, this is Christmas Eve, and as we have no benevolent Christ-child visiting us I intend that my children shall at least have a warm room." The Duke was deeply touched by the simple explanation, and said, „My dear woman, the benevolent Christ-child has already visited me, and brought me a gift which has given me so great joy, that you also shall have a joyful Christmas Eve and shall participate in my happiness." Soon afterwards there appeared at the cottage of the astonished family two ducal servants, carrying two large baskets filled with eatables, fruit, and dainties, and an envelope which contained a banknote for two hundred florins (about £ 20). The Christmas gift to which the Duke referred was Princess Elizabeth, afterwards Empress of Austria, who was born on the morning of that day.

One of the officers of the Court has related the following interesting episode. He says that for some months preceding the death of the Empress disagreeable presentiments had been experienced in certain circles, owing to an incident which occurred at Schönbrunn on the 24th of April of the present year (1898.) The soldier who was posted on sentry duty in a corridor, which is separated only by a glass door from the passage leading to the chapel, came with pallid face and trembling steps to the commandant of the guard, and told him that he had seen the form of a female clad in white and carrying a lighted taper approaching him in the corridor. He at once challenged her, whereupon the figure turned round and returned along the passage; the man followed the apparition, and then observed a light in the chapel. The sentry was so positive concerning the facts which he alleged, that a strict search was forthwith instituted, but without any result.

This incident immediately recalled one of those weird legends that are so common in royal and aristocratic families - namely, that the appearance of a female attired in white presages death or ruin. This particular „White Lady" was seen in 1867, some time before the execution of the Emperor Maximilian of Mexico; again in 1869, immediately before the death of the Crown Prince Rudolf; and, later still, before the drowning of the ill-fated Archduke John Salvator, better known to us as Johann Orth. In Court circles it is positively declared that this dreaded white spectre actually made its appearance at Schönbrunn on the 24th of April.

A statement made by Mr. Barker, the Empress's English reader, who has been already mentioned, tends to increase these feelings of superstition rather than to diminish them. He says that during the last excursion made by Her Majesty at Caux a raven suddenly descended upon the rocky plateau upon which the party were resting, and in passing the Empress its wings brushed her hair. This was looked upon as an evil omen.

Another strange incident is said to have occurred just prior to the Empress's departure for Geneva, which was related by members of her suite. She passed a few days at the Grand Hotel at Caux. On one Friday morning, as she was sitting in the balcony of the hotel, a lady suddenly appeared before the building. She was clad in a white costume with a green bodice. She took a seat under one of the many umbrella tents, and gazed fixedly in a strange manner at Her Majesty. The Empress, evidently disquieted, gave orders that the stranger should be spoken to. Two attendants started to fulfil the order, but the lady disappeared, and in spite of the most careful search, lasting for two hours, she could not be found. In the afternoon the Empress suddenly ordered her departure.

The bed upon which the Empress expired has been sent by the Emperor's command to Vienna; it is made of rosewood, but otherwise it is extremely simple.

The instruments used in the post-mortem examination, as well as those utilised in embalming the body, were burnt in the morgue at Geneva, to prevent any later possible misuse of them.

Dr. Christomanos, formerly reader to the late Empress, has published some extremely interesting reminiscences of Her Majesty. He states among other things that the Empress knew that she was considered an eccentric woman. She remarked to him once, „People ascribe all my eccentricities to my being a Wittelsbach." She often smiled at the poverty of life which crowned heads endure. „How I pity the poor Emperor!" she said on one occasion, „for he has no time to do anything else but attend to the duties of his position."

Speaking of Bismarck, Her Majesty once said: „I think Bismarck was also a disciple of Schopenhauer. He could not bear women - perhaps with the single exception of his wife. He disliked queens. The first time I saw him he was exceedingly stiff. He would have liked to have said" - here she smiled - „The ladies had better remain in their apartments. I think all his hatred of England is on account of the Queen. The poor Empress Frederick has also had to suffer."

CHAPTER XIII.

THE ASSASSINATION.

„It is a very cruel world."
H. Rider Haggard.

In the eighth chapter of this work I have traced the movements of the late Empress from the time that she left Vienna early in the year to her last arrival in Geneva, and it is my sad duty to relate here the terrible crime which ended the life of the sufferer. Had she not deliberately dispensed with protection, it is improbable that the assassin could ever have approached her. Peace be to Elizabeth of Austria's ashes! May she rest indeed! She has, in joining the countless host of the dead, been reunited to her son and brother-in-law, both of whom she loved so well; and to her at least de~'' without doubt a happy release, for life had had noth~ the terrible tragedy of Mayerling. The ~r lonely venerable sovereign at t~ only fervently hope th~' it is difficul* ' visitec

From ti
some ga.
named th
Rue des ~
Street, witi
stands betw~
the middle c
within an irc
Brunswick, wh
the town of Ge~
two lions, lookin

follo
landing
Blanc,
accompanie
beard. When
himself fell to t
Elizabeth upon h
some passengers w
walked to the landing
hardly arrived there whe
with a weak voice she said
unconscious. M. Teisset, a m
Geneva, carried Her Majesty in

122

The Quai itself is adorned with white statues, patches of lawn, and many-coloured carpets of flowers, with trees planted in profusion. Near by is the landing-place of the steamers which ply upon the lake, and a little farther south there is a second landing-stage.

It was on the way from the Hotel Beau Rivage to this stage that, on Saturday, the 1oth of September, at about 12.40 a.m., the Empress was assassinated by the anarchist Lucheni. The Empress had arrived on Friday by steamer from Montreux, in order to pay a visit to the Baroness Rothschild at Pregny, a place celebrated for its magnificent gardens and park. As usual on her journeys, she travelled incognito, and engaged rooms at the Hotel Beau Rivage under the name of the Countess of Hohenembs. The police had no official notice, and therefore no official knowledge, of the presence of Her Majesty. However, the chief of the police department at Geneva, M. Virieux, states that he had, without the knowledge of the Empress, of whose aversion to such regulations he was well aware, placed some detectives round about the hotel at Caux during the last week of her stay there; but in spite of the greatest precautions she noticed that she was guarded, and asked at once that the detectives might be withdrawn, a desire which M. Virieux acceded to.

What really took place is told in the following way by one who witnessed the tragedy:

he Empress was walking, attended by a lady-in-waiting and
ved at some distance by a footman, from the Beau Rivage to the
-stage. When she was near the stage of the Quai du Mont
ere came from the opposite direction a young man,
d by another, who was distinguished by a heavy grey
quite near Her Majesty, the former suddenly threw
r and stabbed her through the heart. The Empress
e ground, but with the assistance of her lady and
o were near she was able to rise again,and
bridge and reached the steamer. But she had
n she seemed to become suddenly ill, and
,What has happened?' and then became
mber of the Chamber of Commerce of
his arms to her cabin after she had

fainted on deck. The captain was reluctant to order his vessel to proceed, but upon the request of the suite of Her Majesty he gave the signal to leave the jetty.

However, very shortly afterwards it was noticed, to the terror of all, that the Empress seemed unable to recover her consciousness. The ladies about her, who had done everything possible to assist the Empress, observed a small spot of blood upon her bodice. Her condition seeming to be serious, the steamer turned back, and a stretcher was improvised of oars and sailcloth, and upon this she was reverently and carefully carried back to the hotel by officers and sailors of the boat."

The wife of the proprietor of the hotel, Frau Mayer, reports the following concerning the last moments of Her Majesty:

„It was two o'clock when the Empress was brought to the hotel, and carried into her bedroom. I was called to give such assistance as was in my power. We took off her clothes, which had already been partly loosened, when we noticed two small drops of blood, and one a little larger of very light red colour: on the body itself there was only a small wound, but no blood was visible. Countess Sztaray exclaimed in consternation, ‚The Empress has been stabbed!' The Empress was lying with a pale face and closed eyes upon her bed. Soon after she arrived in her room she sighed twice deeply: these were the last signs of life. She lay on the stretcher as if asleep, and with no outward show of pain. When we removed her from the litter to the bed she was evidently dead: she must have died when still on the stretcher. Two physicians, Dr. Golay and Dr. Mayer, arrived at this moment, and also a priest; but all remedies proved vain.

The autopsy of Dr. Golay showed some interesting details of the nature of the wound inflicted by Lucheni's weapon. He states that the fatal instrument was driven with such violence (fully 3 1/3 inches in the body) that it broke the fourth rib, pierced the lungs and pericardium, and penetrated the heart from top to bottom, finally coming out from the lower part of the left ventricle. As the weapon was excessively sharp, the bleeding was very slight, and only small drops of blood flowed into the pericardium. So long as this latter organ was not too full, the action of the heart was not impeded: this

123

explains why the unfortunate Empress, even with a wound right through her heart, was able to walk for some distance. But as the pericardium gradually filled with blood death ensued. Had the dagger not been drawn out, Her Majesty would probably have lived some time longer, because as the weapon filled the wound it would have stopped the loss of blood. It appears that Dr. Golay had actually photographed the wound, but was obliged to deposit the negative with the Procurator-General, by whom it was subsequently destroyed. In the opinion of the physicians the death of the Empress was gradual and quite painless.

The weapon which the criminal used was found afterwards in the passage of a house in the Rue des Alpes. It was picked up by the concierge, who thought it belonged to a labourer who had moved from the house the day before, and who, he imagined, had lost it there; and for this reason he did not notify the police of its discovery until the next day. It was a triangular file, which was roughly fastened into a wooden handle, the whole length of the instrument being six and a half inches, a little under four inches being the length of the file. There was no trace of blood upon it, and the point was broken off: the break most likely happened when the murderer threw the weapon into the passage. As soon as the dastardly deed was perpetrated the assassin started to run along the Rue des Alpes, and evidently tried to reach the wide Place des Alpes, where he hoped to be able to hide himself; he was followed by two cabdrivers, Victor Vuillemin and Louis Chamartin, who from their standing-place upon the Quai had witnessed the deed, and who were joined by a sailor, Albert Fiana. Before Lucheni could reach the Place he was overtaken and handed over to the policeman Kaiser, who brought him to the nearest station.

The murder was done in the most cunning way. The assassin had no doubt selected a file, and had converted the same into a dagger of dull metal, well calculating that a bright steel weapon would have soon betrayed his intention; it was in this way that the Countess Sztaray, in spite of her being quite near the Empress, could not see that she had been stabbed, and entirely refused to believe that Her Majesty was wounded till she saw with her own eyes the wound on her body; she and others who were near had up to then been under the impression that the anarchist had simply struck her, and that her fall was due to the powerful stroke.

However we may search the pages of history, we can hardly find a case where such a deed has been committed in the populous centre of a town, during hours when the sun was lighting up the roads with its full summer rays. How pathetic seems the occurrence, when we think of the slim figure, dressed in the deepest mourning, walking slowly along the Quai to reach the steamer, which should have taken her to the place she had selected for quietness and seclusion - who bore no ill-will to any one, and was only desirous of being allowed to enjoy quietly such pleasures as the contemplation of nature could afford her! So full of confidence was she that she refused to allow any precautions to be taken, for her safety. Yet even so gentle a creature could not escape the murderous instrument of the fanatic. How terrible a deed and how far-reaching in its consequences the assassin can scarcely have foreseen. A whole continent mourns the loss of this noble woman, whose life was a linked chain of golden deeds of benevolence and sympathy, whose sole desire was for purity and beauty, who has dried so many eyes wet with tears, and who ever opened her heart to the appeals of all who like herself had borne grief and suffering.

She had arrived ill, but full of hopes; and wherever she went she won the affection and love of all who came in contact with her. But in spite of all she was not permitted to find a peaceful end; nor was she, whose whole life had been a prayer, vouchsafed the last consolations of her religion.

From the statement of the Countess Sztaray we gather the following: „When Her Majesty had regained her consciousness on board the steamer, I asked her, ‚Does Your Majesty feel any pain?' and she replied faintly, ‚No.' She opened her eyes and gazed with gratitude and melancholy sorrow on those near her who were endeavouring to restore her by opening her corsets and loosening her bodice. The only words I heard afterwards were, ‚What has happened?' By this time the steamer had turned round, as Captain Roux feared that the condition of the Empress was serious. Second Officer Gobel improvised a litter, and it was the captain himself, with some sailors, who carried the unconscious lady to the Hotel Beau Rivage, up to the first storey, where the apartments were situated, which she had left only an hour before. Fortunately there was a nurse staying at the hotel, and she, with my assistance and the help of the proprietress of the hotel, took off Her Majesty's shoes and cut up her dress. By this time Dr. Golay had arrived, and he immediately tried artificial respiration, whilst the nurse endeavoured to restore sensibility by rubbing the body of the Empress, which had commenced to grow cold, with eau-de-Cologne and vinegar. All seemed in vain; the doctor made a small incision into the artery of her right wrist, but no blood appeared, which made it certain that she was dead. A priest who had been on the steamer arrived, in order to offer Her Majesty the last consolations of religion, according to the Roman Catholic rites; but he was too late. I believe that the Empress died at the moment that we laid her upon the bed. After her death was confirmed we all knelt down, and with tears prayed to the Almighty for the repose of that noble soul, which must have reached His throne by this time."

As to the assassination itself the same witness says that Lucheni rushed up to the Empress, and seemed to stumble before her; she observed him stretch out his hand, as if to save himself from falling; then she caught the Empress in her arms as she was staggering. The Countess is convinced that the Empress died without knowing that she was the victim of an assassin's weapon.

In another interview with Her Majesty's lady-in-waiting she emphatically stated that she had not seen any weapon in the hand of Lucheni, and that she was under the impression that Her Majesty had only had a fainting fit, due to the heavy blow which the assassin had given her.She had not entertained any fear of serious consequences; in fact, almost up to the last moment she had no idea that the Empress was wounded, and she was unable to see any mark on the bodice. It was only when Captain Roux had expressed his opinion that the condition of the Empress was serious, and had come down into her cabin and cut the corsets of the fainting lady, that it was noticed that she was wounded. He immediately made enquiries as to whether

126

there was a physician on board; but it was found that there was none, and upon that he gave orders to turn back.

It was a strange coincidence that serious apprehensions were felt in Vienna in connection with the Emperor's sudden determination to make a tour through Bosnia and Herzegovina during the course of September, for the purpose of ascertaining for himself whether there were any grounds for the continuous complaints made by the Mohammedan inhabitants against the Austrian administrators in those provinces.

He had been so proverbially unlucky throughout his reign that people in Vienna were labouring under an impression that some untoward event would occur at the last moment to put a stop to the Jubilee festivities organised for next December (1898), and the opinion was freely expressed that it would be quite in keeping with his past career if he were shot down by some murderer on the very eve of the fiftieth anniversary of his accession to the throne.

His life is safe enough elsewhere in the Dual Empire - as, no matter what the political sentiments of the people, they are all united in one common feeling of love and loyal affection for their Emperor. But this loyalty docs not extend to Herzegovina or to Bosnia, provinces which in reality belong to the Ottoman Empire, and which are occupied by Austria much in the same manner as Egypt is held by the English, with the difference that Mohammedan fanaticism in Bosnia and Herzegovina is infinitely more intense and bitter than in Egypt. It must be remembered, too, that a Mohammedan who slays the Christian despoiler of the Caliph is firmly convinced that, far from committing a crime, he is accomplishing a good deed, ensuring his eternal salvation, as well as the gratitude and veneration of all the members of his faith.

An ,untoward event' so much feared by the people of Austria has certainly occurred; the life of the Emperor has not been aimed at, but that of his beloved consort has been taken.

It was in the evening of the loth of September last that the first news of the terrible tragedy in Geneva arrived in Vienna. The detailed official account was not published until Sunday night, the nth. It was

127

pointed out that the assassin, Lucheni, whose name is unknown to any of the police in Europe, most likely bore an alias. It was found that his original intention was to assassinate the Duke of Orleans; but as this proved impossible he resolved to attack the Empress, whom he had followed in her excursions for several days, intending to seize a favourable moment. The cynicism with which he replied to the question of the judicial authorities bordered almost on insanity. He declared on examination that he had seen the Empress four years ago at Buda-Pesth, and immediately recognised her again. He added, „I hope she is dead; that blow did not fail."

It is quite impossible to describe the feelings of despair, rage, and horror which swept over the Viennese when the intelligence of the murder of their beloved Empress became known. They far exceeded in intensity those caused by the news of the death of the Crown Prince Rudolf in 1889. At first no one would believe that such a crime could have been perpetrated, especially considering the character of the victim. When therefore doubt became certainty, the utmost excitement seized upon the masses, who gathered in the streets and public places in thousands, and hurried instinctively to the imperial palace, hoping to hear fresh details. Many people wept aloud, especially the women, who were seen in the streets wringing their hands, and muttering curses against the assassin. In a surprisingly short time the news spread to the outlying districts. The murder of the Empress roused a tempest of fury, such as has scarcely ever before been seen in Vienna. A servant of the imperial house in livery rushed from the palace into the crowd, crying, „Where is the murderer of the Empress?" and fell senseless to the ground.

The first official intelligence came to the Foreign Minister, Count Golukowsky, in the shape of a cypher telegram from the Austrian Consul at Geneva; then followed two messages almost simultaneously, addressed to the principal equerry of the Emperor, from the lady-in-waiting, the Countess Sztaray. The Foreign Secretary drove at once to Schönbrunn, where he found the Emperor making preparations for the autumn manoeuvres in Hungary. The effect upon the venerable monarch when hearing the fearful news was over-whelming; he remained in a kind of stupor for some time.

128

Later on the Emperor said to Prince Liechtenstein, who for years had accompanied the Empress on her journeys as equerry and was much beloved by the imperial pair, „That a man could be found to attack such a woman, whose whole life was spent in doing good and who never injured any person, is to me incomprehensible."

Towards the evening the Emperor drove, amidst sympathising crowds, to the Hofburg. The streets through which he had to pass were crowded, and many angry mutterings were heard when it became known that the assassin was an Italian, and threats were audible among the working classes. Many attempts were made to quiet the growing excitement, and the crowds were told not to throw the crime of an individual on an entire nation.

The Swiss Charge d'Affaires has stated that the Empress was guarded for some time by the Swiss police, but that she had such an objection to this that it had to be stopped. It was an unfortunate circumstance that the Empress was not accompanied in her excursion by any gentleman of her suite, as then the crime might possibly have been prevented.

On Sunday morning the Emperor Francis Joseph telegraphed that he consented to a post-mortem examination. This took place at two o'clock in the afternoon, and we have already given the interesting but melancholy results of Dr. Golay's autopsy.

The body of the Empress Elizabeth, robed in white, was laid the next morning in the triple coffin in which it was conveyed to Vienna. The coffin, which was lined with a profusion of white satin, was placed in a car, converted for the time being into a *chapelle ardente*.

Near the bier was a *prie-dieu* on which lay a rosary and a cross; the floor was covered with a black carpet with flecks of silver, and the walls were draped with black cloth relieved by silver stars. Nuns, sent by the Bishop of Fribourg, knelt beside the coffin. The adjoining rooms were filled with wreaths of flowers, of which a great number had come from Geneva itself Most of them were tied with red and yellow or yellow and black ribbons. Among those who sent floral tributes were the foreign officers attending the military manoeuvres in the neighbourhood.

Reluctantly I am obliged, in order to give a complete history of the dastardly crime, to speak more fully of the murderer himself.He is a young man born of Italian parentage in Paris, but he had never known either his father or mother. At the age of ten he had left the charity school at Parma, in which he had been brought up, and, thrown upon the streets without resources, he had obtained work as an unskilled labourer in order to make a livelihood. At the age of twenty he performed his military service, principally at Naples; on leaving the regiment he obtained a situation as valet to the Prince of Arragon, but only remained in that service for three months. Anarchist ideas began to gain possession of his mind, and prevented his remaining in a state of servitude any longer.

In 1894 the hazard of a life of adventure brought him to Buda-Pesth, where he saw the late Empress for the first time. After long wanderings in search of work he at last arrived at Lausanne, where for the first time he obtained work; it was here that he bought, outside an old curiosity shop, the file with which he perpetrated his crime. He declared that he had not any preconceived idea of the use to which it should be put. In prison Lucheni boasted of his terrible deed; he expressed no repentance, and said it was committed, not to avenge his misery or that of others, which would have been idiotic, but in order that such crimes following one upon another might cause all those arrogant people who fill such positions to fear and tremble. He concluded his statement with the words, „I am an anarchist by conviction.“

During his examination by M. Auberti at Geneva he stated: „I came to Geneva to kill a sovereign, with the object of giving an example to those who suffer and who do nothing to improve their social position; it did not matter to me who the sovereign was whom I should kill. I had heard that the Duke of Orleans was at Geneva, and my first idea was to kill him; but the Duke had left before I arrived. It was not a woman I struck, but an Empress; it was a crown that I had in view. I acted on my own initiative, without any pressure, and I alone am responsible for the deed.“

I need scarcely say that the emotion aroused in Switzerland was almost as intense as that in Austria, and in order to show the horror which the crime had caused amongst the people the Swiss Federal Council organised a great public demonstration of regret and sympathy on the morning of the 12th of September, which proved to be the most imposing affair ever seen in that country.

The famous big bell of the cathedral, known as La Clemence, began to peal at half-past eleven, just as the procession, which had been mustering for some time previously, began to move past the Hotel Beau Rivage. At the head marched a squad of gendarmes with reversed arms, and a few paces after four huissiers in cocked hats and cloaks, half red, half yellow, their leader bearing a mace covered with crape. The members of the Geneva Government came next, headed by President Gavard, and following them a long train of civilians in black, members of the Legislature, municipal authorities, delegates from the forty-seven communes of the canton, deputations from the universities, foreign consuls and consular officials, etc.

The general public joined the procession, which took more than an hour to pass the hotel. The sun was intensely hot, but every head was uncovered. Order was kept by firemen, who wore armlets of black and yellow - the Austrian colours.

All eyes were turned on the terrace of the hotel, where a number of personages in deep mourning were gathered. Among them were General Berzeviczy, Grand Marshal of the Court; Countess Zichy, lady of honour to the late Empress; Count Kuefstein, the Austrian Minister; and other members of the imperial suite, and a priest in plain clothes.

Though the crowd was immense there was no accident and no disorder. The slightest direction of the police commissary on duty was instantly obeyed, and there was a general desire that the demonstration should be characterised by no manifestation of feeling beyond that of respect for the dead and sympathy with the bereaved household and family.

Most of the shops and places of business were closed.

The Emperor of Austria sent the following telegram to the Federal Council, in reply to that of the President of the Federation, in which he had expressed his strong and deep-felt sympathy in the name of the Swiss people:

„Deeply touched by the sympathy expressed in so warm a manner, I thank the Federal Council and the whole Swiss people from the bottom of my heart for their participation in the bitter sorrow which the inscrutable decree of Providence has brought upon me.“

The Austrian Ambassador, Count Kuefstein, telegraphed to the Federal Council at Geneva as follows:

„Count Golukowski has charged me to thank the Federal Council for the cordial sympathy which it has expressed both through me and through the medium of the Swiss Legation in Vienna on the occasion of the death under such tragic circumstances of Her Majesty the Queen and Empress. I am at the same time instructed to convey the most heartfelt thanks, and to inform you that His Excellency will not fail to bring these demonstrations of sympathy to the knowledge of his august master.“

The blessing of the remains in Geneva was carried out, in accordance with a request addressed to the Swiss Government, without military honours. The Federal Council received, both from all parts of Switzerland and from abroad, innumerable messages expressing sorrow and indignation at the crime. This council attended in a body the ceremony, which took place in Geneva at two o'clock in the afternoon of the 13th of September.

Early on the 14th of the same month the special train conveying the body of the murdered Empress started on its long and mournful journey from the place where she had lost her life to the place where her mortal remains were to be laid to their eternal rest.

Before the coffin was finally sealed up the last legal forms were complied with, the identity of the corpse being proved by the presence of the Austro-Swiss authorities. The coffin was fitted with two glass windows, covered with doors, which could be slid back, so as to permit a sight of the contents; these doors were locked - one key was given into the custody of the Master of the Household of the late Empress, whilst the other was handed to the Master of the Ceremonies.

For the purpose of identification the face of the Empress was exposed to view; everybody who saw it was deeply touched by the tranquillity and peaceful expression worn by the countenance of the august dead. The formal certificate of death declares that the passing away was easy and painless.

In the register of deaths in the town of Geneva the name of the Empress is thus entered: „Empress Elizabeth of Austria, Queen of Hungary" (then follows a complete list of her titles and dignities), „sixty-one years of age, died on the loth of September, 1898, at 2.10 p.m., at the Hotel Beau Rivage, Geneva." The entry of the Empress's death stands in the register between those of a child and a woman, who expired on the same day.

The identification or „recognition" having been duly finished, the coffin containing the remains was removed at half-past eight in the morning; the hearse was drawn by four horses, almost hidden by their long black trappings, and was followed by two other cars, each completely covered with wreaths and flowers.

The whole way to the station the streets were lined on both sides by firemen, behind whom were enormous crowds of people, massed many rows deep. The approaches to the hotel had been cleared at an early hour, and all the neighbouring streets were either barred by cords drawn across and firmly fastened or by light barricades. The conduct of the people was, however, everywhere exemplary, rendering the task of maintaining order an easy one.

The coffin, which was almost invisible at the obsequies, owing to the mass of flowers surrounding it, was of polished oak, adorned with raised mouldings and silver fittings and handles. The four feet by which it was supported were also of silver, and the funeral car itself was decorated with ornaments of the same metal. The canopy was surmounted by a silver cross, and at each corner were white plumes fringed with silver. The four horses also bore white plumes on their heads.

The coffin was brought down from the *chapelle ardente* and placed on the car by eight bearers, immediately after which the *cortège* was formed, a force of gendarmes and firemen acting as escort.

Among the wreaths upon the hearse itself were tributes from Queen Amalie of Portugal, the Queen of Roumania, the inhabitants of Geneva, and others from various Swiss cantons. Those on the two cars following included wreaths from the Swiss Federal Council, the Council of State, the consular body in Geneva, the Italian colony, various political associations, the Spanish colony, the ladies of Geneva, the Comte de Montholon, the French Ambassador to Switzerland, and the foreign military attaches present at that time in Geneva for the annual manoeuvres.

Immediately behind the two floral cars came a large number of closed carriages, two abreast, those on the right containing the representatives of the Emperor and the personages of the Austrian Court sent from Vienna, and those on the left the members of the Swiss Federal Council, headed by the President and Vice-President of the Confederation, the horses being all decked with black trappings.

By the side of each coachman was seated a Federal usher, dressed in a scarlet pilgrim's robe. All the official mourners wore black with white ties.

The occupants of the five Austrian Court carriages were as follows:

First Carriage: Count Bellegarde, Grand Master of the late Empress's Court; and Countess Harrach, Her Majesty's Mistress of the Robes.

Second Carriage: General Berzeviczy, the Grand Marshal of the Austrian Court; and the Countess Festetics, lady-in-waiting to the late Empress.

Third Carriage: Count von Abensperg-Traun, Grand Chamberlain of the Austrian Court; and Countess Sztaray, the lady-in-waiting who was with the Empress when she was assassinated.

Fourth Carriage: Mr. Barker, the late Empress's Greek reader; and M. Paoli, the French police functionary who was always appointed to accompany Her Majesty when travelling in France. Fifth Carriage: Count von Kuefstein, Austrian Minister to Switzerland; and his Secretary of Legation, Baron Giskra.

Other carriages followed with members of the Empress's suite and a number of her personal attendants. Another detachment of gendarmes and firemen brought up the rear. During the passage of the procession

134

from the hotel to the station, which was reached in a little less than a quarter of an hour, the great bell of the cathedral, known as La Clemence, tolled continually. Not only were the roads along the route taken by the procession thronged with people, but every window of every house commanding a view of the *cortège* was filled with people anxious to pay their last homage to a good and noble woman. Nevertheless, the procession passed by in the most absolute silence, every man's head being uncovered, and numbers of women crossing themselves devoutly as the coffin passed.

The main hall of the Carnavin Station, through which the coffin had to pass on being transferred from the hearse to the special train, had, by the directions of the Jura-Simplon Railway Company, been converted into a large mortuary chamber, the walls being draped with black, while the floor was tastefully arranged with a large number of palms and other foliage plants. The entrance to the hall was also hung with black draperies, from amid which, over the doorway, the Austrian imperial eagle stood out boldly on a white ground.

As the remains were removed from the car a benediction was once more pronounced over them by the chief ecclesiastic of the cathedral. The coffin was then borne to the special train which was to convey it to Vienna, and was placed in the carriage which had been arranged for its reception. The only wreaths placed in the car with it were those sent by the Queens of Portugal and Roumania, and those of General Berzeviczy and Countess Sztaray. As soon as these had been arranged the doors of the car were closed and hermetically sealed, after which the Swiss civil authorities passed in turn before the group of Austrian dignitaries who were to travel by the train to Vienna, and gave them a farewell salute. The Emperor's representatives then took their places in the saloon-car. An adjoining carriage was occupied by several high railway officials.

In the meantime the remaining wreaths and flowers from the hearse, and those from the two cars which followed it, had been conveyed to the carriage reserved for them. This was next to the engine, and following it was the special car with the Empress's remains; next came a carriage occupied by servants, two salooncars for the members of the Court and their suites, a dining-car, and a brake.

All the Swiss Federal authorities remained on the platform until the train started, the Austrian representatives at the same time standing on the platform of their saloon-car, and again exchanging salutes with them as the train left.

The day before the crime the Empress had visited Baroness Julia Rothschild, wife of Adolphe Rothschild of Paris, at Pregny. Some days previously an intimation had been sent from Caux of the intended arrival of the Empress on Friday, the 9th, to take lunch at Pregny. Baroness Rothschild proposed that she should send her yacht, which would come via Caux and Territet direct to Bellevue, without obliging Her Majesty to touch at Geneva. The Empress declined this kind offer, but on the day fixed she appeared with Countess Sztaray at the Baroness's villa. She had left her carriage some distance from the gates, and had walked the rest of the way; she was in excellent spirits, and spoke to the steward of the estate, with whom she had become acquainted on a former visit. After lunch, at which a band played, a walk was taken in the splendid park; Her Majesty led the way with the Baroness, conversing with her in French. The Empress especially admired the orchids, which were then growing in great quantities in the hot-houses, and the Baroness offered to send her a bouquet, which Her Majesty accepted. The Empress then returned to Geneva. It is a pathetic fact that these orchids formed part of the magnificent wreath laid by the Baroness on the coffin of the Empress.

In closing this chapter I may refer to the enormous number of telegrams of condolence received by the Emperor. Even from the remotest parts of the world, such as Africa and Australia, came sympathetic messages. The Queen of England was one of the first to telegraph:

„Words fail me in which to express my heartfelt sympathy and my horror. It is too dreadful, too cruel. May God support and protect you.

Balmoral, September 10th 1898.   *Victoria."*

The German Emperor expressed his feelings in the following words:

„Deeply shaken and still unnerved, I can scarcely find words to say how I feel for you, and how I suffer with you in sorrowing over your

heavy loss. It is a trial from Heaven that we mortals cannot understand, which only weighs us down with fearful severity. The only consolation for us poor human creatures is that it is ordained."

King Humbert telegraphed:

"The cruel misfortune which has struck you fills us with shuddering and indignation. I wish I were near you to show you by my affection the share I feel in your pain. Margherita and I join with all our hearts in your prayers and fears, praying God to afford you that consolation which He alone can give."

The Czar and his consort sent the following message:

"We are horrified to receive such dreadful and unhappy tidings. In this cruel trial we would express to you our sincere feelings of sorrow and pain. May God sustain you and lend you strength to bear this irreparable loss!

Alexandra and Nicholas."

A message was also sent by the Lord Mayor of London to this effect:

"The Lord Mayor desires in the name of the citizens to express the deep indignation and sorrow felt in the City of London by all classes alike at the terrible crime that has deprived Austro-Hungary of her Empress-Queen and its august ruler of his beloved consort."

To these wires may be added one from the President of the United States:

"I have heard with profound regret of the assassination of Her Majesty the Empress while at Geneva, and tender Your Majesty the deep sympathy of the Government and people of the United States.

William McKinley."

Among the many wreaths and other floral tributes with which the coffin and its surroundings were crowded was one which was enveloped with the American colours and had the following inscription on its ribbons: „From the President of the United States: a tribute of heartfelt sympathy, in memory of a noble and gracious lady." There was also a silver palm branch, which was placed on it in the name of M. Felix Faure, and a coronal in that of the Government and the Republic.

137

CHAPTER XIV.

AT REST-OBSEQUIES IN VIENNA AND UNIVERSAL MOURNING.

„Only the actions of the just
Smell sweet and blossom in their dust."
Shirley.

The 17th of September, 1898, will ever be remembered by the thousands and thousands who thronged the Austrian capital to pay their last tribute to their murdered Empress. It was a beautiful autumn day, the sun appeared in all his splendour, not a cloud was visible in the deep blue sky, when the Empress Elizabeth was placed in the tomb of her ancestors. Nature, whom she had loved so dearly, seemed to have put on her most lovely garb.

It was about ten o'clock at night on the 15th when the body of the Empress reached Vienna by the railroad which is called, after herself, the „Elizabeth-bahn." Never since Austria won for herself a name among the nations of the earth, has the homecoming of any of her sovereigns proved so mournful or impressive as this - the last journey of the accomplished and beloved Empress Elizabeth. From city to city the funeral train rolled slowly onwards, accompanied by the tears and orisons of the deeply afflicted people, who once warmly welcomed her as a blushing young bride, and today bemoan the loss of the beneficent lady who lessened their sorrows and intensified their joys during the most eventful period of the century. In Innsbruck, in Hall, in Salzburg, in a word all along the route taken by the *cortège* the entire population, their houses draped in mourning, their persons clothed in deepest black, and their hearts full of love and sympathy for the gallant and disconsolate old Emperor, turned out to pay the last honours to their idolised Empress. A representative of the united Swiss railways had escorted the imperial train to the frontier, and at three o'clock on the morning of the 15th had reached the loyal province of Tyrol, where, despite the early hour, crowds assembled at the station, and literally covered the space around the hearse with fresh-cut dewy flowers. In spite of the orders which had been given to keep the platforms clear of people, it was impossible to prevent the sorrowing subjects from doing reverence to the beloved dead. Crowns and garlands of flowers were laid round the coffin by various corporations and public bodies, and that offered by the entire population of the province was woven of palms, lilies, and white roses, and bore simply the legend, „Tyrol to its dearly beloved Empress."

The Court ceremony, which took place at night, although suggestive in its details of the days of Philip II. of Spain, and even of the more ancient times of Byzantium, had for its aim and object the delivery of the Empress's body by her own Master of the Household to the chief Court officers of the Emperor.

Vienna had become completely transformed. The flagstaffs on either side of the spacious Ringstrasse, from the tops of which the national colours had been gaily floating ever since the official inauguration of the Jubilee, were now covered with crape and white muslin, and immense black flags hung from their summits like eerie shadows. The sky had become overcast with dark drifting clouds, rain seemed imminent, and the black scowl of heaven harmonised with the soul-harrowing sorrow of the people.

There was a great exhibition of peculiarly tasteful and appropriate expressions of the national sorrow - wreaths and other tokens in roses, laurels, palms, and crape. So numerous were the black flags floating from roofs, windows, and balconies, that all Vienna appeared as though darkened by the countless wings of some mighty monster, enthroned aloft in undisputed power. Shortly after the body had arrived at the station, the Emperor and his two daughters, the Archduchesses Gisela and Valerie, left the palace at Schönbrunn, and started off in a closed Court carriage for the chapel at the imperial residence. The party arrived there shortly after the remains had been placed on the bier, and all three knelt down before it, where they remained in prayer for some time.

139

The appearance of the Emperor at his Vienna residence had been quite unexpected, and his last parting with her who had been dearer to him than life itself was emotionally tragic. He had driven through by-ways and side-streets, and had arrived within the precincts of the historical palace unnoticed by the countless multitudes who blocked the thoroughfares leading to the Hofburg. His Majesty stood erect and silent in the vestibule, where he was joined by Prince Leopold of Bavaria and the Archduke Francis Salvator, his son-in-law. From time to time he changed his position uneasily, raised his head higher, compressed his lips, and made evident but successful efforts to subdue the terrible emotions which were struggling within him for the mastery. His two daughters, who were close by, were completely overcome and quite unable to restrain their tears. How long the brave old monarch would have been able to master his harrowing feelings it is impossible to conjecture, but after a few minutes of most painful suspense the eight coffin-bearers ascended the stone steps and approached the vestibule. Leaving his place, the Emperor drew near them; and they, riveted to the spot by the sudden apparition of the sorrowing monarch, stood still. This was one of the most painfully dramatic scenes of the night - this sad and silent and final meeting after a short parting of the two who had been everything to each other. The Emperor remained motionless, as if rooted to the ground, his dry eyes fixed upon the plain dark brown coffin, his hands shut. Every person who took part in this moving scene, except perhaps the two Archduchesses, presented the appearance of figures cast from a mould, or of human beings thrown by some supernatural agency into a trance.

After two or three minutes of this silent contemplation, the Emperor, raising his hand, gave the signal that the coffin should be taken to the chapel, he himself following with head erect, eyes dry, and the noble bearing which has ever been one of his principal characteristics. Princess Gisela had mastered her feelings to some extent, although she still continued to weep and sob; but the Archduchess Valerie tottered, and had to be gently led by her husband. The members of the imperial family were followed by the personages who had accompanied the Empress's body from Switzerland, and then the ceremony of blessing the body began.

The vested priest stood in the centre of the mediaeval chapel, which was draped in black. The coffin was laid on the bier before the altar, a large silver crucifix at the head, and four crowns, once worn by the murdered Empress, at the opposite end. During the simple but impressive rite, which lasted a quarter of an hour, the Emperor remained standing, while the august ladies knelt on *prie-dieus*. The words of the service, familiar to every Roman Catholic, and exceptionally so to the Emperor, struck, now that they were uttered on behalf of his beloved consort, upon the tenderest chords hidden deep in the sorrow-stricken heart, and the emotions he felt produced a twitching of the facial nerves, an uneasy movement of the fingers, a convulsive movement of the lips, which no effort could hide. The priest's voice grew more solemn and impressive; and when at last he pronounced, in tearful tones, the name Elizabeth, Francis Joseph's eyes filled with tears, which ran in torrents down his cheeks, the gallant, erect bearing vanished, and he was now a sore-stricken, broken man, who stood weeping and sobbing in the presence of his murdered and beloved wife. The monotonous tone of voice in which the sacerdotal blessing was continued exercised a calming effect upon the Emperor, who again recovered his apparent composure.

This ceremony over, Count Bellegarde, the Chief Master of Ceremonies of the Empress, delivered up the keys of the coffin to Prince Liechtenstein, who occupies a similar position in the Emperor's Court. Francis Joseph, turning his eyes towards Prince Liechtenstein, saw the keys, and then, moving mechanically towards the coffin, like one in a dream, suddenly stretched out his arms towards the remains of the murdered Empress, and with a look of inexpressible anguish fell heavily upon his knees, and let his head fall upon the undraped lid of the coffin, which he passionately, convulsively, and repeatedly kissed, helplessly, hopelessly sobbing aloud the while. This extremity of grief, for which there is no medicine upon earth, affected every one present, and there was no longer a dry eye in the chapel; the Archdukes, Prince Leopold, the priests, and servants all gave vent to their grief in tears.

A few moments later everybody withdrew except the Emperor, his daughters, and his sons-in-law, who laid garlands on the bier, and then knelt down before the altar, where they remained five or six minutes in prayer. Rising from his place, the Emperor gave a sign that all were to retire. As he was leaving the chapel His Majesty noticed Countess Sztaray, who had been the Empress's companion in her last travels. Turning to this lady, and speaking in a loud, clear, unfaltering voice, he said, „Did Her Majesty suffer much?" „I think not," was the reply; „for Her Majesty soon fell into a deep and painless sleep, and with but one sigh was released from life." The Countess Sztaray seemed overcome by the painful reminiscence, and sank helpless on her knees. His Majesty took her hands and raised her up, after which all the persons who had taken part in this memorable drama retired.

Upon the general desire of the people, the Emperor consented that the remains of his beloved wife should lie in state for two days in the imperial chapel, which is in itself mediaeval and mystic, but much too small for such ceremonies as this, which had brought together no less than eighty princes, as well as countless throngs of people exhibiting signs of the greatest grief. The walls were draped in black, their sole ornament being the Empress's coat of arms, with the inscription, „Elizabetha Imperatrix Austrae, 1898." The atmosphere was heavy with the scent of numberless flowers, mingled with that of incense. In the centre of the chapel was a plain dark brown wooden coffin, without any pall, containing the metallic shell in which she who was lately the Empress of Austria and the Queen of Hungary sleeps her long last sleep.

Slender green palms, tasteful garlands and wreaths, symbolical of mourning, of victory, of hope, filled the centre of the chapel, and formed a pleasant and reposeful contrast to the ubiquitous black. Two nuns were kneeling in silent prayer like two wax figures, apparently lifeless. On the steps of the bier stood four warriors, as motionless as statues; they were the guard of honour, whose brilliant armour reflected the sea of light, whose waves inundated the little church. Marvellous and vision-like were the effects of the play of colours of the precious stones that ornamented the four crowns lately belonging to the murdered lady: the crown of Empress, first worn by Marie

Theresa; the crown of Queen, used at her coronation in Buda-Pesth more than thirty years ago; the crown of Archduchess; and that of Princess. On a cushion hard by were exhibited the nine decorations which Her Majesty possessed, conspicuous among them being the Order of the Sternkreutz and the Catherine Order of Russia; and on another cushion were placed a pair of white gloves and a fan. Before the coffin only three wreaths were to be seen; they had been laid there by the loving hands of the august lady's consort and children.

The funeral took place on Saturday, the 17th, at four o'clock in the afternoon.

The streets through which the *cortège* passed were enveloped in a cloud of sable mourning, and looked like dismal corridors leading to some vast abode of the dead. Sorrow was the predominant note, even among those classes of society whose horizon seems usually circumscribed by the present and who are devoid of an outlook upon the future or the past.

Obsequies in Vienna and Universal Mourning 355 Flowers were everywhere offered for sale - forget-me-nots, white roses, graceful lilies - all of them enveloped in transparent crape. The naked flames of the burners in the lamp-posts on the road served as torches, and the garish light burnt steadily in the breathless air from mid-day onwards. The grim silence of the crowds was continually broken by the clatter of gorgeous carriages, conveying the notabilities of Austria to the imperial palace; kings and princes, field marshals and admirals, chancellors and prime ministers, cardinals, archbishops, and monks, followed each other in rapid succession, attired in a variety of uniforms, costumes, and robes, representative of past ages, and of many existing secular and religious institutions.

At a quarter to four the body-servants of the deceased Empress removed the coffin from its standingplace, whereupon the Court chaplain recited once more the traditional blessing. After this the coffin was placed in the historic hearse, which, within the short span of a hundred years, has carried the remains of three Emperors and six Empresses from the Burg Capelle to the Capuchin Church. It was drawn by eight colossal raven-black steeds, over whose heads were nodding plumes of black ostrich feathers. The coffin, once laid on the

143

richly carved hearse, which was surmounted by a black crown, was effectually hidden from view by the dense black falling drapery. The coachmen and other attendants were dressed in black, and wore three-cornered hats over their white wigs. Not another light hue or colour was anywhere to be seen in their liveries. Everything in and near the hearse was as black as the four ebony pillars that supported the roof of the lugubrious vehicle.

The funeral procession was led by Polish Uhlans, with drawn sabres glistening in the stray sunbeams that straggled athwart the floating black flags. Then came a rider attired in quaint costume, as black as the hearse. Another squadron of Uhlans, followed by another sable cavalier, and then a long line of mourning coaches, each one drawn by six black horses, conveyed the palace dignitaries, including those ladies who were in the service of the late Empress. This melancholy monotony of unchequered black was all at once succeeded by a vision of gay colours, such as might suit the day of a monster military review - cloths of gold and silver, stuffs of scarlet, plumes of snowy horsehair, and polished steel, glistening in the sun. The palace guards, the body-guard riders, and others, with bright red, gold-spangled coats, battle-axes, and quaint headgear, rode onwards. Next appeared from beneath the triumphal arch a stream of yellowish light, proceeding from the flambeaux of the torch-bearers, who surrounded the imperial hearse. The vehicle of the dead was followed at some distance by brilliantly dressed cavaliers, hussars, and palace guards, but not by the monarch himself, nor by any of his noble guests, all of whom had already left the Hof burg by a different route for the historic church of the Capuchin friars.

The Capuchin Church is probably the plainest place of worship in all Vienna. Of very limited dimensions, devoid of all architectural and other ornament, it was built in high-souled humbleness of heart by the Empress Anna, the consort of the Emperor Matthew, in the beginning of the seventeenth century, for the express purpose of serving as the burial-place of the members of the House of Habsburg. The distinguished lady who founded the monastery was the first whose remains were laid in the dismal vaults below, and the Empress-Queen Elizabeth is the last but one who will be interred

144

there, for there is now no room for more than a single coffin, that of the reigning Emperor, and even before that can be laid in position the casket of the Emperor Maximilian will have to be removed. The vault can contain one hundred and twenty-eight coffins, and that of the late Empress is the one hundred and twenty-seventh. Very narrow are the precincts of that house of prayer and death, but infinite is its grasp of weal and woe, and in the darkness of its dismal vaults has been quenched the light of the life-dreams of many a scion of the historic House of Habsburg. It was constructed for a less numerous company of the illustrious dead than that which now occupies its hallowed space and from time to time it has been enlarged.

So soon as the hearse reached the little whitewashed church the body-servants of the Empress removed the pall and revealed the coffin to those who were near enough to see it. It is a narrow plain oaken shell, the corners bound with silver, and its only ornament is a silver cross on the lid. Every other member of the House of Habsburg was conveyed thither in a heavy massive coffin. The reason of this difference is that the coffin in which the Empress Elizabeth rests is a foreign shell, made under exceptional conditions. The moment it was raised aloft from the hearse the word of command was given to the soldiers, whereupon, to the beating of muffled drums, accompanied by the low tones of wind instruments, the lowering of crapecovered flags, and the presenting of sabres, the troops offered the last military honours to the illustrious dead.

Meanwhile the coffin had been carried through the door into the sombre church. This humble place of worship, which is never very bright, was literally covered with black cloth and crape, which served as a powerful foil to the white episcopal mantles in which the bishops were clad and the glittering gold of the sacerdotal copes. More than eighty bishops were crowded together in the circumscribed space allotted to them in front of the high altar. In the midst of these „spiritual shepherds" stood Cardinal Archbishop Gruscha of Vienna, whose melancholy duty it was to pronounce the final benediction and utter the last solemn words. The Imperial Court Choir, whose voices were to accompany that of the Cardinal, and chant the thrilling Libera over the lifeless remains, was presided over by Hans Richter. Word

145

having been brought to the Emperor, who, with the other members of the imperial house, was in the refectory of the Capuchin Monastery, His Majesty, in time to meet the coffin, entered the church by a side door to the right of the high altar at a few minutes past four. He was followed by the Emperor William and other monarchs, while the Crown Princess Stephanie and the two daughters of the Empress, enveloped in robes of mourning, moved forward. The Emperor manfully mastered his feelings. All eyes were riveted upon him as he stood erect in front of the coffin. At a short distance there was a long crape-covered bank, on which the Emperor William, Prince Leopold of Bavaria, and Kings Albert of Saxony, Charles of Roumania, and Alexander of Servia took their places in the order named. Opposite the Emperor Francis Joseph stood the Papal Nuncio.

The subdued sounds of church bells and the tones of muffled drums which penetrated from without suddenly ceased, and the silence was as that of the graves underneath. Then Cardinal Archbishop Gruscha, raising his voice, recited in solemn accents the funeral benediction, whereupon the choir chanted the traditional *Libera,* which, being translated, means, „Deliver me, O Lord, from everlasting death in that awful day when the heavens are to be shaken and the earth, and when Thou comest to judge the world." The refrain, which contains the terrible words, „Dies irae, dies illae" is peculiarly impressive; then comes the softer and more hopeful passage beginning, „I am the resurrection and the life." The last words were pronounced, and silence reigned once more. The Head Master of the Ceremonies, rising, approached the Emperor, and with a profound obeisance signified that the last and saddest moment had arrived - that of the eternal leave-taking from that which once was near and dear. The attendants lifted up the coffin, and the Emperor, with his daughters and sons-in-law, followed. The foreign princes bowed low as the mortal remains of the Empress were carried past them to the vault below. Signs of acute pain passed over the Emperor's countenance from time to time, but they vanished as rapidly, leaving no trace. Once, and once only, during the recital of the benediction, composed of Biblical texts, the natural echo of whose solemn oratory is a sigh, the monarch seemed on the point of breaking down; but his iron will maintained the mastery. Now, while he descended to the house of death below, fears were entertained that his energy would abandon him, and the silence was painful in the church, where every prince and priest and warrior listened for a tell-tale sound from the depths beneath.

An eye-witness of what took place in those subterranean spaces declares that, when the coffin was laid in the provisional resting-place, the Emperor, accompanied by Cardinal Gruscha and the Father-Guardian of the Capuchins, knelt down on a *prie-dieu* and prayed.

The old Austrian custom is no longer observed of giving the body of a dead monarch to the Capuchin Church, the heart to the Augustinian Church, and the intestines to the Metropolitan Church of St. Stephen. The last personage whose mortal remains were thus divided was the Emperor's father, Archduke Francis Charles.

The sorrowing Emperor, resting his head on the *prie-dieu,* remained silent and motionless for seven or eight minutes. Then the form of the prostrate monarch quivered, and choking sighs, subdued sobs, and half-suppressed moans were heard; a cold convulsive shudder ran from man to man throughout the vaults, and the clergy, familiar with death in all its aspects and sorrow in all its degrees, wept and sobbed like children.

A few seconds later the Emperor himself once more was seen entering the church. He signed to the Emperor William to precede him in leaving the house of worship. As he neared the door he cast a longing, lingering look in the direction of the gloom-girt vault, wherein sleep so many who have helped to make Austria's history, among whom the last will take a foremost place as one of the few of the dead whose works are active forces still and whose names burn bright as stars. Not for a long time after the departure of the Emperors did the other members of the illustrious company retire; nor did the general public disperse until night had descended, with darkness denser than all the black flags of mourning.

Soon after the funeral of the Empress, in reply to a question put by the Hungarian Prime Minister (Baron Banffy), the Emperor said, „Do

147

not grudge me work. On the contrary, I am minded to work harder now - the one consolation that still is vouchsafed me."

Memorial services were held in almost all the capitals of Europe. The one in London took place at the Church of the Immaculate Conception, Farm Street, and was an extremely solemn and impressive ceremony; the interior of the building was heavily draped with black cloth, and a cloth-covered catafalque was placed at the upper end of the nave near the sanctuary rails.

The nave was reserved for the Corps Diplomatique and others especially invited by the Austro-Hungarian Embassy. Among the foremost of the mourners were the Duke and Duchess of York, the former being in naval uniform, and the Duchess wearing black with a long veil of crape; Princess Christian, attired in deep mourning; and the Marquis and Marchioness of Lorne. Representing Her Majesty the Queen, came the Earl of Pembroke; while Lord Suffield, Colonel Egerton, and General Bateson attended on behalf of the Prince and Princess of Wales, the Duke of Connaught, and the Duke of Cambridge. The Lord Mayor brought with him the sincere sympathies of the citizens of London.

Needless to say, there was also a large gathering of diplomats; each embassy sent its group of representatives. Russia, Spain, and Turkey were represented by the Ambassadors themselves. Portugal, Denmark, Belgium, Servia, Sweden, China, and Siam were all represented by their Ministers. In the absence of Count Hatzfeldt the delegates from the German Embassy were Count Hermann Hatzfeldt, Baron von Eckhardstein, and Herr von Oppell; while for France M. Geoffray was present. The United States, Italy, Holland, Greece, Roumania, Japan, Peru, Chile, and Persia were also among the countries who had representatives present. Chopin's Funeral March and Beethoven's famous Funeral March on the death of a hero were rendered on the organ with great solemnity.

A funeral service was also held in Paris, at which H.R.H. the Duke of Connaught, attired in the full uniform of his high military rank, was present. The President of the Republic, who, owing to the Cabinet Council at the Elysee, was unable to be present in person, was represented by General Hagron.

Not the least interesting funeral service was the one held at St. Patrick's Chapel, Maynooth College. Thirty-three priests and six hundred and thirty students were present, as well as a number of neighbouring residents, including Sir Gerald Dease, Lady Dease and her sister, the Honourable Miss Throckmorton, who had been for many years attached to the suite of the late Empress of Austria, and many others.

The signs of mourning were universal, the navies of the world hoisting their flags half-mast on the day of the funeral.

This chapter may be closed with a short *résumé* of Her Majesty's will, to which a peculiarly mournful interest is attached, as it was only completed three months before her death - namely, on the 20th of June, 1898; and it opens with the remarkable sentence, „One never knows what may happen."

It is pretty well known that the Empress possessed a very large fortune and income in her own right, but it is not very generally known that Her Majesty's collection of jewels was not only unique but in many respects considered to be one of the finest in Europe. A large portion of the collection, to the value, it is stated, of over £ 600,000, is to be sold, and the proceeds are to be applied to various religious and charitable purposes. There are several special jewels which are to descend as heirlooms to the imperial family, amongst these being the Golden Rose presented to the Empress by Pope Pius IX. Nearly all that the Empress had in her own power to leave she bequeathed to her grand-daughter, the young Archduchess Elizabeth, daughter of the late Crown Prince Rudolf.

CHAPTER XV.

CONCLUSION.

„The grief that all hearts share
grows less for one."
Sir Edwin Arnold (Light of Asia).

Such a work as the present, which endeavours to delineate the character of a most admirable and unique woman, could hardly be deemed complete if it did not give at least a short sketch of the man to whom she was married, whom she loved with great sincerity, whom she admired, and to whom she has been all in all.

Francis Joseph I., Emperor of Austria and Apostolic King of Hungary, was born in 1830, and ascended the throne of his ancestors on the 2nd of December, 1848. He is a grandson of Francis I., the father-in-law of Napoleon I., and therefore a nephew of the Empress Marie Louise. His mother was a Bavarian princess who was much in the hands of the Jesuits, and influenced his earlier education unhappily. The events of the memorable year 1848 were too much for the feeble-minded Emperor Ferdinand, who was then on the throne, and he abdicated; his brother and heir declined to accept the vacant crown, and so he handed it on to his son, then eighteen years of age, young enough to be moulded to the new ideas.

The early reign of the Emperor was full of troubles, worries, and vexations. The Hungarian revolt had to be suppressed, and he shared in person in the storming of Raab, a strong fortress in Hungary, at which time he received a slight wound. In the complicated struggles in Germany which followed the events of 1848 he joined Bavaria and Württemberg in opposition to Prussia, and it was only due to the interposition of the Czar that war was prevented. In 1852 his life was attempted, but he was fortunately saved by his equerry and a citizen. In 1854, as we have seen, before he was twenty-four, he married his

150

first cousin, the subject of our memoir, who was then a little more than sixteen years old.

During the Crimean War the Austrian Emperor remained neutral, and was reproached with ingratitude by the Russians, as the Czar had helped him to put down the insurrection of Hungary five years previously.

The New Year's Day of 1859 brought a shock to Europe that must have disturbed the Emperor Francis Joseph considerably. At the reception of the foreign ambassadors in Paris, Napoleon pointedly said to the Austrian representative that he regretted his relations with his master were unsatisfactory. A few weeks later war broke out between Austria and France in alliance with the then kingdom of Sardinia; Austria being defeated, the Emperor made peace, conceding Lombardy to the new kingdom of Italy. At this time Germany was weary of its feeble confederation, which had become only nominal. Unification had been in the minds of all Germans for many years, but it had remained a dream because the smaller states were without power, and Austria and Prussia were opposed to and jealous of each other.

At last in 1863 the Austrian Emperor, relying on his personal popularity, took a bold step: he summoned all the German rulers to meet him at Frankfurt-on-the-Main, where so many of his ancestors had been crowned, and asked them to discuss the future of Germany. With one exception all obeyed the summons of the scion of the Caesars, and it must indeed have been the proudest moment of Francis Joseph's life when he saw them rally round him. Unfortunately the exception was the King of Prussia, who had appointed Bismarck his Minister about this time, and who had remained deaf to the entreaties of the princes that he should join them. The consequence was that the meeting was abortive.

At the end of the year came the war with Denmark, over a question which was popular with the German people. Although Austria had little interest in it, she could not refuse to take it up as Prussia did so, and she was obliged to join in the contest, lest her rival should have all the credit of fighting for a popular cause. Two provinces were taken from Denmark; the victors quarrelled over the spoils, and the strife ended in the Seven Weeks' War of 1866, in which the Austrian arms were most disastrously defeated. The Prussians came down from the North almost to the walls of Vienna, whilst the Italians attacked in the South. The peace which followed was made on terms that were most generous to the losing side: Austria lost Venice to Italy and recognised the supremacy of Prussia in the North German Confederation.

In all this series of defeats neither Emperor nor people lost honour; the Austrian armies were as ready to fight after defeat as before, and the people adhered to their unsuccessful Emperor with the same affection which in the subjects of Francis I. had excited the envy of Napoleon I. To the country itself the disasters proved beneficial; the Emperor became a great constitutional reformer, and in this way he affords a most interesting instance of a man in whom such wide changes of ideas took place. As we have already mentioned, he was brought up at what was most probably the most bigoted Court in the world, under the iron rule of the Jesuits, proud and exclusive, absolute, autocratic, despotic to a degree - a Court where feudalism was paramount, and where the lower classes were looked upon as mere tools. The son of a weak father and a narrow-minded mother, he had become sovereign of a great Empire when only eighteen years old, and within twenty years we see him one of the most enlightened monarchs, turning from feudalism and autocracy and becoming an absolutely liberal constitutionalist.

With the exception of the occupation of Bosnia and Herzegovina, during which he was compelled to employ force, peace has reigned for many years in the realms of Francis Joseph, and he and his Government have made good use of it. The sovereign is second to our Queen in length of reign, but not in labour for the good of his people, and it would be a very difficult task to decide which of the two is the more popular amongst their subjects.

The relations existing between Francis Joseph and Elizabeth through the forty-four years of their married life were most friendly, and no serious disturbances of their conjugal peace occurred. After the Empress had retired from Court life, and had taken up her abode more or less frequently abroad, her spouse visited her from time to time, and frequently spent weeks with her. On those occasions they were generally observed walking without any suite and engaged in most earnest conversation; it may well be said that their mutual love and esteem lasted undiminished to the end of Elizabeth's life, and therefore we can well understand the unspeakable grief which has been caused to the venerable monarch by her violent death.

But not popular only in his own country, this sovereign has won the esteem and love of most foreign countries, and the sympathy shown him in this his last terrible trial was so universal as to be entirely unique; this is proved by the extraordinarily large assembly of foreign potentates and princes at the funeral obsequies of his wife. There stood the Emperor William of Germany, accompanied by General von Hanke; and with a large suite the venerable King of Saxony. The Kings of Roumania and Servia; the Duke of Saxe-Coburg-Gotha (Duke of Edinburgh); the Grand Duke Alexis of Russia; the Prince Regent of Bavaria; the Crown Prince Constantine of Greece; the Crown Prince of Italy; the Crown Prince Danelo of Montenegro; Duke Nicholas of Württemberg; the Hereditary Grand Duke of Saxe-Weimar, and he of Oldenburg; Duke Charles Theodore of Bavaria, and his wife and daughters; the Hereditary Grand Duke of Baden; Prince Ferdinand of Bulgaria; Prince Albert of Belgium; Prince Christian of Schleswig-Holstein, accompanied by Lord Denbigh (who is a scion of the House of Habsburg), as representative of Her Majesty the Queen of England; the Duke of Alençon; and the Dukes Rupert and Christopher of Bavaria, were also present. The President of the French Republic was represented by General Faure-Biquet; the Queen of Holland sent Baron Werner-Palland, and the King of Sweden Count Gyldenstolpe. The Duke of Cumberland and the venerable Queen of Hanover, who both happened to be absent at the time, were also represented. There had arrived representatives from Brunswick, Schleswig-Holstein, and Hesse-Darmstadt; and the German Chancellor, Prince Hohenlohe, was present in person.

It will be seen, when looking through the list of these illustrious personages, that there was an assembly of princes the like of which perhaps has never been seen in this world before. As a matter of course, too, the members of the imperial family were present. The

153

Crown Prince's widow, with her daughter, the Archduchess Elizabeth, visited the coffin early on the day of its arrival in Vienna and laid wreaths upon it, the youthful daughter of Rudolf being so overwhelmed with grief that she had by force to be drawn away from the coffin.

It would be impossible to enumerate the list of telegrams of condolence in this work. I have given some of the principal ones verbatim in the last chapter, and I may add that a very long one arrived from Pope Leo XIII., others from Queen Christina of Spain and the President of the Swiss Confederation. Besides these some were received from the German Empress; the Queen of the Netherlands; the Queen of Italy; Sultan Abdul Hamid; the Kings of Denmark Saxony, and Württemberg; the King of Portugal and his consort; the King and Queen of Sweden; the Mikado of Japan; the Queen of Belgium; the King and Queen of Greece; the King of Siam; the Grand Duke of Hesse; the Grand Duke of Weimar; the Grand Duke Peter of Oldenburg; the Grand Duke of Mecklenburg-Strelitz; Leopold, Prince Hohenzollern;

George, Duke of Saxe-Meiningen; the Duke of Saxe-Altenburg; the Prince of Montenegro; the Princess of Bulgaria; John of Mecklenburg; Charles Gunther of Schwarzburg-Sondershausen; the reigning Count of Lippe; the Sultan of Zanzibar; the Khedive of Egypt; the Presidents of the Republics of Peru, Uruguay, and Chile; etc.

It has been decided in various towns to erect memorials or monuments to the late Empress by public subscription. In Buda-Pesth a very large amount of money has already been collected for the purpose.

The universal sympathy which was shown on the occasion to the bereaved monarch has no doubt been a source of great consolation to him, and he replied to all those who forwarded sympathetic addresses in words of sincere gratitude. I need only give the message received by the Lord Mayor of London in answer to the telegram sent to the Embassy - a letter from Count Albert von Mensdorff, Austro-Hungarian Chargé d'Affaires:

„Austro-Hungarian Embassy,
Belgrave Square, Sept. 19th, 1898.

My Lord, - I have not failed to convey to His Majesty the Emperor and King, my august master, the kind expression of condolence that your Lordship has sent to this Embassy on behalf of the City of London.

I have now the honour to inform you, my Lord, that I have received the orders of my gracious Sovereign to express to your Lordship and to the citizens of London His Majesty's sincerest thanks for and high appreciation of their kind sympathy. I have the honour to be, my Lord, your obedient servant,

The Right Hon.	*Albert Mensdorff,*
the Lord Mayor of London	*Austro-Hungarian*
	Chargé d'Affaires."

It shows the enormous sense of responsibility and duty of the deeply afflicted Francis Joseph that he expressed himself at once to the effect that he would attend to the State affairs without interruption. He left shortly after the funeral for a long stay with his daughter the Archduchess Marie Valerie at the Castle of Walsee, whence he went to Gödöllö in Hungary; he remained absent for some time from Vienna, in order to regain the calm so necessary to him after his recent great distress of mind. Meanwhile the Emperor had given orders that the apartments of his late consort should remain undisturbed.

I stated in a former chapter that the weapon of the murderer and the surgical instruments used by the Swiss physicians in making the post-mortem examination had been burnt in Geneva by order of Francis Joseph, who has acted in this in accordance with rule and old-world usage and tradition. It is a custom which is based partly on superstition, and partly on a determination to prevent articles of this kind from falling into the hands of dealers in curiosities, or being on exhibition in some more or less reputable museum.

EMPRESS ELIZABETH OF AUSTRIA.

*Although it has been impossible for me in this memoir
to do full justice to the dead Empress, yet I hope that I
have succeeded in giving a sufficiently true sketch of
her late Majesty to show that, whatever may have been
her eccentricities, her character was one of the most
lovely and noble this century has seen. She is dead, but
her memory will live for ever.*